C000276990

Us Kids

by Carole Anne Stafford & Alan Crowe

(Growing up in Ladywood, 1945 - 1960)

Qu̇ercuS

****
QuercuS
John Roberts
8 Hillside Close, Bartley Green
Birmingham B32 4LT
0121 550 3158
****

Us Kids
(Growing up in Ladywood, 1945 - 1960)

by Carole Anne Stafford
and Alan Crowe

© Carole Anne Stafford and Alan Crowe

ISBN 1 898136 15 7

First Published 1998

Front cover photographs:

Carole at ages 10, 16 and today, taken by family and friends.

Back cover:

Top right - The Nelson pub in Sandpits (Mitchell and Butler), one of the main non human characters in the book.

Top left - The Lyric Picture Playhouse on the corner of Edward Street and The Parade was the local fleapit. It was once a Methodist chapel but is thought to have opened in 1909 as the Queen's Theatre, putting on music hall and animated picture shows.

Bottom - the other corner of Edward Street, in which Carole's father established his sheet metal working business.

These three photographs were taken by Mr Victor J Price of Hall Green, local historian, writer and kind gentleman, who lent us the prints gladly and at short notice. They appear in his book *Old Ladywood* (Brewin Books) which contains many more pictures and much interesting detail about the area.

Other photographs were taken by members of Carole's family and friends.

Preface

QuercuS specialises in publishing books about the western Midlands, or the area between the rivers Trent, Severn and Avon that geographers call the "Midland Triangle". Titles include *Midland Woods & Forests, Midland Rivers, Midland Ghosts & Hauntings, Midland Castles, Historic Houses & Gardens, Heart in my Boots, Coaching Days in the Midlands, Midland Murders & Mysteries* and albums of pen and ink sketches of buildings in Hales Owen, Bromsgrove and Birmingham. And coming soon is *Midland Spirits & Spectres*

Alan Crowe persuaded his partner, Carole, to collaborate on a book about her growing up in Ladywood, and it was in manuscript when they started looking for a publisher. They got wind of me from the shelves of Smith's in Halesowen and I took to this book immediately, in fact the unfolding story is so absorbing that I found it difficult to put down because it is told as a series of vivid and dramatic scenes.

The Authors

CAROLE STAFFORD - this whole book is about Carole who describes herself inside and out, so what more can we add here? but we should say more about the ghost writer, scene painter and midwife of this book.

ALAN CROWE was born in Balsall Heath, Birmingham in 1942. A Magic Lantern for his 7th birthday kindled an passionate interest in all things cinema, and most of his working life was spent selling cine cameras. Amateur film making has been Alan's life long hobby, but aspirations to make block busting, all singing, all dancing screen epics were frustrated by 'too much time spent in the billiard hall'. Problems with his eyesight brought early retirement and presented the opportunity to shape some of Carole's early memories into a book, having decided that a film version was beyond amateur resources. With Carole, Alan runs a film/video group in Halesowen, making and showing local interest movies.

One Author's Excuses

"What me write a book? Don't be so bloody daft!" It takes me long enough to read a book, let alone write one, and I even had trouble filling in the form to join the library. But then it was explained that I would not really have to write it, just talk into a tape recorder. Well, that was different. Talking is something that I'm good at, too good, some people say. But I do have a good memory for things that happened a long time ago.

When it comes down to it, I still blame Flint McCullough and Major Adams for my inability to put pen to paper. I spent too much time watching programmes like *Wagon Train* on telly and not enough on my school homework, usually no time at all. And when that handsome scout and the grizzled wagon boss rode off in to the sunset, quitting our TV screens forever, they left me to struggle with the mysteries of spelling and grammar for the rest of my life.

On the radio the other day I heard a famous author say, "All writers are liars, they call on their own experiences but then invent, embroider and exaggerate in order to make a better story..." I have consciously tried not to do this, and I don't think that I need to. Where I have quoted dialogue it must be remembered that I heard conversations like these many times over the years, in one form or another. Most of the incidents I describe are also well remembered by my sisters and brothers. Even now, on the rare occasions that we get together, we amuse each other with talk of 'the old days' in Ladywood, and laugh about things that were not quite so funny at the time. This has helped to keep my own memories fresh.

Looking back through the pages I hope that I haven't portrayed mom and dad as unsmiling tyrants, because they certainly weren't. Mom was a popular Saturday night pianist at the pub and a keen member of the ladies darts team, earning the nickname "double top". Dad loved our days out in Blackpool or Stourport and was always ready with a wisecrack. I don't think we ever watched a TV western without him saying at least once, when a cowboy or indian fell dead, 'Well, now 'e can goo an' get 'is wages and geroff 'ome.' There was plenty of laughter as well as tears in our house.

All that I can hope is that these scenes from my early life re-
kindle some of your own childhood memories, and you may
think, "Yes, that's just how it was." Or if it was different
for you, perhaps I can give you a glimpse of another sort of
childhood, not all good, not all bad, just different. I often
used to regret that I never learned to speak or write what they
called then 'the King's English', but technology has come to
my rescue. So, with a little help from my friends, here goes...

Carole Anne Stafford
Halesowen
August 1996

Dedication

To Mom and Dad - who always did their best for us, and
to Jade and Bryn who will only have to read about it.

Money, Money, Money

Money in Carole's early life was pounds, shillings and pence,
but we decimalised our currency in 1972 so many people never
experienced this strange system. In the book we have shown
modern values in [square brackets], but in brief - 12 pennies
made 1 shilling, 20 shillings made 1 pound, so a shilling was
the same as our decimal 5 pence. The coins in circulation were
the halfpenny [.02p], the penny [.4p - or about half a modern
penny], the sixpence (or tanner) [2.5p], the shilling [5p] -
also known as a 'bob', a two shilling piece [10p], and the half
crown piece worth two shillings and sixpence [12.5p]. Above
this came the 10 shilling note [50p], but Carole rarely met any
of these.

Ah yes, I remember it well... did I ever tell you about the
time .. Hell, I'm getting old.

John Roberts
QuercuS

Sandpits

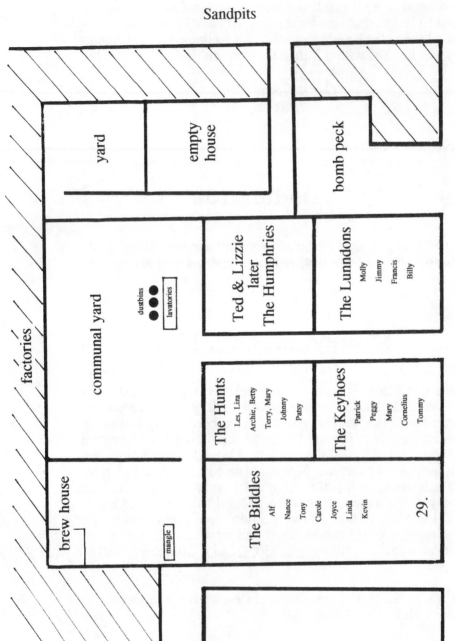

yard

empty house

bomb peck

factories

communal yard

dustbins

lavatories

Ted & Lizzie later The Humphries

The Lunndons

Molly
Jimmy
Francis
Billy

The Hunts

Les, Liza
Archie, Betty
Terry, Mary
Johnny
Patsy

The Keyhoes

Patrick
Peggy
Mary
Cornelius
Tommy

brew house

mangle

The Biddles

Alf
Nance
Tony
Carole
Joyce
Linda
Kevin

29.

Nelson Street

1. 29 Nelson Street
2. Nelson Inn
3. Junior School
4. Clements' junk shop
5. Goodman's Haberdashery
6. Lyric Picture Playhouse
7. Dad's first factory
8. Traffic island with tree
9. Barbara Bennet's house
10. Granny Graham's house
11. Denis's house
12. Marshall's Grocers
13. The Edward pub
14. Veronica's house
15. Hickman's Greengrocers
16. Rogers' Pork Shop
17. Fazackerley's Chip Shop
18. Railway Club
19. 'dead cat'
20. Greek Orthodox Church
21. Raggy Rowley's yard
22. The Red Rec.
23. Doctor's Surgery
24. Billy Butts' clothes shop
25. runaway pushchair
26. Alexandra Street house
27. The Ice Rink
28. Bulpitt's (Swan) factory
29. Pawn Shop
30. Elim Tabernacle
31. Library

1.

2.

3.

1. Carole aged about 8 with
rag hair ribbon.

2. Aged 10, the 'Chinese' look.
The top button was a victim of
the dreaded mangle.

3. With Dad at Blackpool c1955.

4. Aged 16 after leaving home.

4.

Four Ages of Carole

Contents

The Magic Fork   1
Early Days in Nelson Street   3
Two Up, Two Down and an Attic   5
Everybody Needs ...   14
My Dad the Gaffer   16

A Birthday and a New Arrival   19
Friday Night Friends   24
Rob Dogs, Good Dogs and Other Shopping Problems   25
Veronica   31
Kevin   35

Granny Graham's Garden of Rest   41
Did you ever see such a thing in your life?   45
Another Brother   49
Lost, Stolen or Strayed   54
Sunday, Bloody Sunday.   63

A Sixpenny Sick Note   72
Blind Eyes in Nelson Street   75
Back Trouble   80
The Gas Man Cometh   83
Sitting on the Ice in the Ice Rink   85

Teacher's Rest and Mother's Pest   88
Love, Death and Rock 'n' Roll   93
The Big School   104
Things I Didn't Know I Didn't Know   108
When Nelson Got his Eye Back   120

Up in the World   122
"I like riding in my car... "   129
These Dangerous Years   133
Of Boys, Booze and Babbies   137
Certificate X   144

Hi Ho, Hi Ho   153
Soldier, Soldier   155
The Ring and I   157
Going Where the Sun Shines Brightly   163

The Magic Fork

It was the usual Monday dinner time scene in our little house.
We were all seated around the table, elbows resting on pages
from the *Sunday Pictorial* which protected the new white table
cloth. An interesting smell wafted over as Mom lifted a steam-
ing enamel pan from the stove. She put it down on the sports
page in front of Dad and he helped himself to a large plateful
of Mom's home made stew and dumplings. Stew was always
a good way to use up any leftovers from Sunday dinner but
it was a regular favourite in our house, with most of us.

Mom served herself, then began ladling out stew to us kids:
my younger sisters, Joyce and Linda, me and Kevin the 'babby',
who was still in his high chair. We grabbed our metal spoons
and started to break up the dumplings to let out some of the
heat, but there was still one empty place at the table. Suddenly our back gate crashed shut, and the jangle of a bike being
propped against the wall and a jaunty whistle told us that 'old
big ead' was home. This was our elder brother Tony, who was
almost 13 and liked to show that he was a cut above the rest of
us kids by coming in a few minutes late for dinner. This was
something that Dad would not tolerate from the rest of us. 'In
on time or goo without', was his rule.

Tony walked into the kitchen twirling his bicycle clips around
one finger. As usual, he looked quite pleased with himself, but
as he caught sight of the familiar white pan, the superior smirk
fell from his lips. Now he put on his well known hard done by
expression,

"Oh no!", he groaned. "Not bloomin' stew agin."

What happened next was all Tony's own fault. It had been building up for days; we all knew that. Every dinner time he would
come in five minutes or more late, look at what was on offer and
say something like, 'Errr, don't like that. Can I 'ave a boiled
egg instead Mom?', or 'Y'know I can't stand that rotten cabbage.
Can I 'ave beans on toast instead?'

To keep the peace and avoid having Tony sulking through the
meal, Mom would get up and oblige. Dad had been taking in
these performances but saying nothing, sometimes flicking hard
glances towards Tony, or puffing out his cheeks in exasperation

1

and jabbing a fork viciously into the meat on his plate. Us kids all noticed, we saw all the signs; only Tony seemed un-aware that Vesuvius was about to erupt.

Hardly had 'Not bloomin' stew agin' died away, when in one swift movement, almost too quick for the eye, Dad jumped up, grabbed the empty chair and brought it crashing down on Tony's head. Bits of the chair broke away and scattered across the table as Tony fought to keep his feet, hanging on to the table edge to keep from falling. Dad thrust his face down to Tony's level. His cheeks were red, his eyes started from their sockets, an expression that we had all come to know and dread.

"If I've gorra fuckin' eat it, you've gorra fuckin' eat it."

With that, he sat down and calmly got on with his stew. Although we had been expecting it, we were stunned by the suddenness and ferocity of Dad's fury. Tony, with as much dignity as he could muster and a red lump rising on his forehead, lifted the remains of his chair, sat shakily down and began to eat without another word. Spoonful after spoonful he munched, chair bits and all, his eyes rolling and his hand shaking. I dared not look up or catch Joyce or Linda's eye. To giggle now would surely bring down Dad's wrath on the head of the giggler, and there were untouched chairs around. No, keep my head down and concen-trate hard on the stew, try to get through the rest of the meal without laughing out loud.

Fortunately for Tony, the chair in question was one that Dad had made himself from odd bits of wood, so it did him less damage than a shop bought one surely would. Dad was handy at making things. He had also made the table that we were eating off, but that survived a few more weeks until another meal time upset. My sisters and me did manage to get through that meal in one piece, and when we finally shot out into the yard, we celebrated Tony's sudden downfall with wild shrieks of delight. It was about time 'old big' ead' got it, we all agreed. He was a bit quiet for a couple of days and had trouble putting on his school cap until the lump on his head went down, but he quickly got back to his usual cocky self. I do not remember him ever again complaining about stew for dinner.

The drama of Tony and the chair is one of my favourite memor-ies of the Nelson Street years, so I have put it at the start of the book. It is typical of the sort of thing that often happened in our house, especially at meal times, and usually as Dad was about to plunge his fork into the potatoes that were always piled high on his plate. In fact, these dinner time dramas cropped up so often that I began to think Dad had some sort of magic fork. One wave over his dinner was enough to conjure up trouble.

Anyway, I now have to go back and put down all those boring details about who we were, where we lived and how we got there. More mayhem coming shortly.

Early Days in Nelson Street

Why is it that whenever I think about the time that I was born, I get this image of Dad sprawled in the gutter? I know what you are thinking, but it was nothing to do with drink. The story Mom told was that Dad got so excited when I was born, his first daughter, that on his way to the hospital he fell off the tram. True or not, I always enjoyed the story. I was born on 30th May 1945, shortly after VE day. The honour fell to Loveday Street Hospital, Birmingham, and although there is no blue plaque, the building has survived as the Dental Hospital.

In the dim and distant past there was a French queen, called Carole with an 'e'. I never knew this, but my Gran on my mother's side apparently did, for it was she who suggested the name for me if I turned out to be a girl. I could not ask my Gran about her knowledge of French history because she died shortly after I was born. But I was christened Carole Anne, both with an 'e', which Mom thought made them just that little bit posher. Mom had been christened Annie May but for some unknown reason was always known as Nancy. She was born in a tiny back to back terraced house in the Ladywood area of Birmingham. Many years later I found out that Ladywood was then considered one of the roughest areas in the City, a slum in fact, although I never knew the word or realised what it meant until I was 11.

Mom had lived all her life at number 29 Nelson Street just off the Parade, along with her parents, four brothers and two sisters. It is hard to imagine now how nine people lived in a house that was classed as a 'two up and two down'. To add to the problems, my Grandad had established an ironmongery business in the front room. But years passed, kids grew up, married and moved away. Mom was the last child at home and still in her teens when my Grandad left the family home never to return. To make ends meet Gran had to close the ironmongery business and take in lodgers.

One day, a young chap called Alf Biddle came to their door in search of lodgings. His father had recently died and his mother had remarried but he could not get on with his new step father. He was just 14 years old and Mom would often tell me how she had taken an instant liking to the new lodger.

"'E was ever so clean, always went out ter werk and yer know 'e looked just like Frank Sinatra with all 'is mop of black 'air."

Alf Biddle had fallen on his feet, for Frank Sinatra was Mom's favourite singer.

It turned out that young Alf Biddle was a keen picturegoer, as was his landlady's daughter, Nancy Mitchell. They soon started to go to the local flea pits together, in fact they started courting. They would go to the Lyric Picture Playhouse in Edward Street or up to the Crown Super Cinema in Icknield Port Road. Sometimes they would get dressed up and go to the Odeon or the Scala in the City centre. It was on one of these trips, after they had seen a Doris Day and Frank Sinatra double bill, that Alf told Nancy she looked just like that famous star (Doris not Frank), and asked her to marry him. They got married on a snowbound Boxing Day in 1940 and lived with my Gran in that tiny house in Nelson Street.

By this time Dad had completed his apprenticeship as a sheet metal worker and was in what they called a reserved occupation. This meant that he was not called up for war service, but Mom told me he did his bit as an Air Raid Warden, patrolling around the district and shouting at people who left their lights on. He also did firewatching from the roof of a local factory, stamping out incendiary bombs with his work boots as they dropped around him. It was not until years later that I saw an incendiary bomb in the Science Museum and realised that Mom was slightly exaggerating Dad's prowess as a firefighter.

When in that spring of 1945, Mr and Mrs Biddle took their first daughter, Carole Anne with both her 'e's, home to Ladywood, there were already two other residents at 29 Nelson Street. One was my brother Tony who had been born two years earlier during the war, and the other was an old lady called Flossie. She had been one of my Gran's lodgers and Mom had not the heart to throw her out when the old lady died. Besides, Flossie's rent money came in useful when she remembered to pay it.

Two Up, Two Down and an Attic

My earliest memory is the loud popping sound that the gas light made when it was lit. It always made me jump, but when I was little the gas lights fascinated me. Thin metal chains with rings on their ends hung from the ceiling on either side of the gas pipe. Pull one ring to switch the gas on, the other to turn it off. The flimsy gossamer like bag that gave out that harsh yellow light was called the mantle, and I often wondered how such a fragile thing could stand all those hours of burning. When the mantle was finally ready to give up the ghost, the flame would turn to a pretty blue colour and the hissing sound became louder.

I also remember the feel of cold lino under my hands and knees as I crawled around our tiny kitchen. I would stare through the black metal grating of the fire guard into the glowing embers, or amuse myself picking at the peeling paint on the oven door. For years Mom cooked all our meals on the old, blue mottled gas stove which had seen better days, but nobody could remember when. Next to it was a brown stone sink with a wooden draining board and a single tap for cold water. There was a wooden table with four hard chairs, and beside the fire grate, an old armchair covered in cigarette burns. I soon got used to the smells of stale cooking, bleach and stale urine. I grew up thinking everybody's kitchen stank like ours, and around our way most of them did.

From the kitchen a dozen rough, stone steps led down to the coal cellar. From about the age of 5, the winter months for me meant frequent trips down into the damp and inky darkness to haul up buckets of coal or put pennies in the gas meter. To do this, I had to feel about on that cold metal box for the tiny slot, then force the coin home and turn the flat little handle until the penny fell with a hollow clunk. The floor of the cellar was always inches deep in coal dust with lumps of coal scattered everywhere.

At first the coalman's regular deliveries frightened me very much. As he tipped sacks of coal through the grating under our front window, the whole house would shake and there was a terrible rumbling sound. Later on it became one of my jobs to count the sacks of coal as he lifted them from his horse drawn cart. Mom was always very particular about this.

"You mek sure you count eight bags, I don't trust that bugger.", she would tell me.

To me the coalman was a frightening sight, completely black
from top to toe, his head covered by a big leather cap worn
backwards so the long peak protected his neck from the heavy
sacks. White circles around his eyes made him look like a half
made up minstrel, and when it rained the water would draw grey
stripes down his face, just as if he had been crying. Even his
sad looking horse was shiny with coal dust and I could not
understand why anybody would want to do such a job. I knew
for sure that if I was the coalman's daughter he would
never get a kiss from me when he came home.

The only other room on our ground floor was at the front of
the house, the best room as Mom called it. It was strictly out
of bounds to us kids because this was where Mom kept all her
treasures. Most of them were items left to her by my Gran, but
there were also presents from Dad in their courting days, prizes
Mom had won playing darts and lots of souvenirs from forgotten
'charabang' trips to the seaside. They were all things that Mom
considered too good for everyday use, and Gran's old china
cabinet with glass doors was full of such trinkets. There was a
Chinese teapot with gold letters which read - 'A Present from
Barmouth', a tiny Blackpool Tower in a glass globe of water
which snowed when you shook it, and a Welsh lady in a black
hat whose apron turned red in fine weather and green when
it rained. There were fancy vases that never knew flowers,
chalk ash trays that never needed emptying, and slim, red
sherry glasses that never touched alcohol.

An old, upright piano stood against one wall hiding a ragged hole
in the plaster. Mom told me that the keys were made from real
ivory, whatever that was. It had been the prized possession of
her father, my mysterious Grandad who had walked out all those
years ago, not even bothering to take his beloved piano. I never
found out why, but the fact that it seemed to weigh about a ton
may have had something to do with it. My own favourite item
in the best room was the wind up gramophone which stood on
a polished wooden cabinet full of old 78 rpm records.

Often, when I helped Mom clean and polish the best room, she
would play a record or two and I would wind the shiny metal
handle. This was my introduction to music and I was thrilled and
captivated by the sounds coming from the dark depths of the big
brown horn. The music was thin and tinny and the voices sang
through a noise that sounded like bacon frying, but I didn't care.
Perched on a chair staring down into the horn with my head on
one side, I must have looked like the HMV dog as I tried

to sing along, only half understanding the rattling words. It was here that I first discovered Donald Peers, Gracie Fields, Vera Lynn and Hutch. But although I loved the music, I did not want to be like any of those famous singers of the day. Even then I knew very well who and what I wanted to be, and by the time I was 6 I could do an impression of my favourite, George Formby, using an ornamental barometer from Bournemouth as my ukulele.

> "Ladies' nighties I have spied,
> With men's pyjamas side by side,
> I've often seen what goes inside,
> When I'm cleaning windows....."

I understood hardly a word, but window cleaning sounded lots of fun. A few years later this particular chore came my way and I changed my mind.

A narrow flight of stairs from our kitchen led up to two small bed rooms. Tony and me slept in our cots in one and Mom and Dad in the other. When Joyce and Linda were born we all slept in an old double bed until Tony was 8 or 9, when he moved up to the attic. Although number 29 was classed as two up and two down, we did have the tiny attic as a third bedroom. It was not a nice place; there was no fire grate or gas light, and just one tiny window right under the eaves. The whole house was damp but the attic was worst of all, with mildew sprouting in the high corners and green fungus creeping across walls and ceiling. For Mom and Dad, decorating our house was like painting the Forth Bridge. No sooner had they finished distempering the walls of the attic than patches of damp and green fungus would start to stain the new wallpaper in the kitchen.

We had no hot running water, no inside toilet and no bathroom, but just outside the kitchen door and hanging on a rusty nail was an old tin bath. Every Friday night Dad would drag this in front of the coal fire and almost fill it with cold water, then add a few kettles of hot from the gas stove to make it a bit less unbearable. Dad was always first in to use the clean and reasonably warm water, then Mom, then us kids. Kevin, the 'babby' came next, being the smallest and thought to be the least dirty. Last of all, after much struggling, splashing and cursing from Dad, came Rex the dog, but he did not seem to mind too much.

Our kitchen door opened directly onto a roughly paved yard that we shared with the five other families in the block. At the far end were four brick lavatories that we also shared, but

without door locks. You had to be a good singer to avoid embarrassment if you lived in our yard. A trip up the yard to the 'lavvy'
on a cold winter's night was something none of us could face, so
the dreaded slop bucket came into use.

These were of white enamel with matching lids and stood beside
our beds for emergency use only. Since Mom and Dad's went
out drinking nearly every night of the week, in their case it was
always an emergency. Every morning the slop buckets had to
be emptied, and when I was about 6 years old, Mom put me in
charge of the slop pail patrol, as we called it.   Of all the jobs
I was saddled with over the years, the slop pail patrol was the
worst. The buckets were heavy and smelly, and had to be hauled
downstairs and the full length of the yard to the lavatory block.
It could be a long and slow journey as Mom and Dad's bucket
was usually full to overflowing, and I would have to go steady
to avoid spillage and a clout round the ear. I usually tried to
get the slop pail patrol over as early as possible before the
other kids in the yard were up and about. Otherwise I would
have to run the gauntlet of their abuse as I staggered up the
yard clutching a white bucket in either hand, like some
tipsy milkmaid.

'Yah, Carole Biddle tekin' yer Dad's piss out. Err, we can smell
it from 'ere...' Don't even answer them back, just keep walking -
I mean staggering. 'Don't drop any on yer shoes will yer? It'll
rot 'em. Yah, Carole Biddle...piddle...piss pot.' I would rather
have scraped out the inside of the oven any day.

There was another small, brick building in our yard which was
known as the 'brew 'ouse', and that is just what it had been,
somewhere for brewing your own beer. In my day it held a
copper boiler over a fire grate to boil water for the weekly
wash. By the start of the 1950s most women in the block did
their washing in the kitchen sink or, if they had sheets and
blankets, outside in the yard using the tub and 'maid'. This
was a wooden contraption like a stool on a long handle which
was used to bash the dirt out of the clothes. The brew houses
gradually became wet weather play places for the yard kids,
a place to park your bike or to keep pigeons or chickens.

Just outside the brew house stood the mighty mangle, another
survivor from days gone by but still in regular use until the mid
1960s. It was a great cast iron contraption with huge, powerful
wooden rollers designed to crush every last drop of water out
of wet washing. At an early age it became another of my

8

little jobs to feed dripping clothes and sheets to the rollers and snatch away my fingers at the last second while Mom struggled to turn the iron handle. While she did this she would sometimes tell me horror stories about little girls who had not been paying enough attention to what they were doing and failed to remove their fingers in time. These stories made a deep impression on my young mind, so that for years afterwards I was continually on the lookout for girls with flattened finger ends.

The trouble with the mangle, apart from its power to maim you, was that it not only crushed water out of the washing but everything else that passed through it. Dad would often moan about his work shirts, all neatly washed and ironed but with only fragments of buttons down the front. I still have an old school photograph which shows me smiling happily, with the large top button of my dress looking like a half eaten biscuit, another victim of the dreaded mangle.

Mention of the mangle brings back memories of washdays. Every Monday morning the blank, brick walls that hemmed in our yard and the higher factory walls that overlooked them, were hidden from view by row after row of wet washing. If it rained, as it always seemed to, the washing might stay out for days on end until it was as dirty as before washing. In winter, our wet clothes would be stained by sooty lumps and the black smoke that drifted from hundreds of house chimneys. Another washday hazard was the steam trains that rumbled under St Vincent Street. The top end of Nelson Street would vanish behind clouds of smoke and steam, and moments later I would watch fascinated as millions of little black specs floated over the yard walls and attached themselves to the wet washing. Mrs Bradshaw would have wept.

The front door of our house opened straight onto the pavement of Nelson Street. Our side was lined with rows of two up and two down terraced houses, and some had even been divided into two at some stage. This meant that some families with four or five kids were forced to live, if you could call it living, in a house only half the size of ours. On the other side of the street, the row of grim factory buildings was broken only by the rusty iron railings of Nelson Street Primary School, which all us kids attended from the age of 5 until we went to 'the big school' at 11. Our school was only 30 yards away but we were always pestering Mom to let us stay for school dinners. Even now I don't know why, perhaps we were just curious. We had never eaten school dinners, we never even saw what school dinners looked like, but whenever we brought the subject up Mom would say,

"Yer not eatin' that fuckin' rubbish. You'll come 'ome an' 'ave a proper dinner".

But I think the real reason was that she could not afford the 3 pence [1.25p] weekly for each of us.

Looking along Nelson Street towards Saint Vincent Street we could see the little traffic island with its scraggy tree, the only greenery for miles. Beyond this we could see the trams droning their way along Kings Edwards Road into the city. Looking in the other direction, the skyline across the busy main road was dominated by a Greek Orthodox Church. This was (is) quite a handsome building despite the years of smoke blackening its red bricks. It looked best when covered by a heavy fall of snow and I would imagine that it was the fairytale castle that I had seen in *Sleeping Beauty* at the pictures.

On the far corner of the street facing the Parade was the Nelson Inn, where Mom and Dad and most of our neighbours drank every evening they could afford, and on many when they could not. In those days there was a pub on every street corner, and in some of the longer ones like Ledsam Street there were three or four. We were surrounded on all sides by dozens of small factories engaged in one of the many metal bashing trades for which Birmingham was world famous. Walk down any street in Ladywood and you would struggle past piles of galvanised buckets, motor cycle mud guards, bike frames or aluminium wash tubs, or any of the thousand and one metal items that were manufactured locally.

The noise, smoke and smells from these factories were with us all day, and often all night. The sickly sweet smell of machine oil and the harsh stench of burning metal were ever present, and when the sun shone in Nelson Street, the air would be full of glittering metal particles drifting out of workshops and in through our windows and doors. So the women of our street, and all the surrounding ones, waged a never ending war against 'the dirt and filth'. It was a war they could never win and did not expect to, but at least a good fight had to be put up; that is, if you wanted to be 'respectable' in the eyes of our neighbours.

To Mom and most of the other women, 'respectability' was all important, and there were fairly strict rules. The man of the house always went out to work to support his family, you never got behind with your rent, daughters were always safely married before getting pregnant (or at least, before the baby was born). Most important of all, you scrubbed your front step clean with bleach at least twice a week. Falling down on any of these unwritten rules meant an immediate loss of the prized respectability and you were liable to get yourself talked about. This was something to be avoided at all costs.

"Hey Nance, you sin 'er kertins at number thirty fower?"
"Nah, worrabout 'em?"
"Like bleedin' rubbin' rags they are. S'posed ter be white."
"Ah, an' she ain't done 'er front step fer fuckin months."
"Dirty cow! 'Ave yer noticed 'er gell's puttin on a bit o' weight lately?"
"Oh well, she's bin gooin with that insurance feller an' we all know what 'e's after don't we?"
"Insurance feller? I dain't know 'e was an insurance feller."
"Oh yeah, I've sin 'im. Sticks 'is bike clips in the belt of 'is mac when 'e teks 'er up the entry..."

Needless to say, everybody fell down on these rules of respectability at some time or another and everybody got themselves talked about. Of course, everybody talked about everybody else, but, and this was the important thing, you always talked about people behind their backs. In this way you never really got to know if and when you were being talked about, or the sordid details of the gossip. The quickest way to quell interest in your own sins was to dig up, or think up, an even juicier item about someone else. And so it went on, with gossip about everything from a dirty front step to mass murder being passed from yard to yard. As time went by the names changed, but certainly not, as they used to say the old American TV cop series - Dragnet, to protect the innocent.

As I grew older I began to realise that it was not just too much booze, too many kids or even too little money that was the major blight on the lives of the families who lived in Ladywood in the 1940s and 50s. The overriding factor was the awful dilapidated condition of the houses. Our rent was paid to Birmingham City Council, but when it came to repairs, renovation and decoration, tenants were usually left to fend for themselves. I do remember one visit from council workmen who painted half way up the yard and lavatory walls with a white distemper. A man with a bowler hat and clipboard told us that the distemper contained DDT and would 'deter the vermin'. Well, if the vermin were deterred they put on a brave face and did not let it show.

On every wall and ceiling in our house there were muddy patches where the plaster had crumbled to dust. This damp plaster was a

fertile breeding ground for all kinds of creeping, crawling and
flying 'critters', as we called them. Cockroaches ran nightly
races across our bedroom floor and up the walls. Us kids would
amuse ourselves by burning them off with lighted candles. There
were things in the bedclothes which I now know were fleas and
bed bugs. In our innocence we wondered why they always looked
bigger in the mornings, swollen and reddish coloured. We would
crush them under our thumbs with a loud popping sound, not
realising that the red stains left on the walls were our own
blood.

Then we had damp and fungus, mice and rats, black beetles
and silver fish. But apart from this, everything was all right.
The point I want to make is that us kids did not know enough to
be disgusted or outraged by our living conditions, we accepted
them as normal, as a part of everyday life to be endured with no
complaints. We considered ourselves a 'clean' family, but however clean you were, however much you washed, however much
you tried to decorate or scrub or sweep, however many mouse
traps you set or critters you stamped on, sooner or later the
conditions would start to grind you down.

A lot of families just seemed to give in, living from day to day
and crisis to crisis, all made a little less unbearable by regular
doses of Mr Ansell's tonic taken in pint measures. Mom and Dad
liked their drink but never put it above the welfare of us kids.
They never gave up the struggle to better our living conditions
in any way they could.

"Nance, we gorra get out of this fuckin' ole.", Dad would often
say with an edge of despair in his voice.

But he had a dream. Dad's dream was that one day he would have
his own sheet metal business, a passport out of Nelson Street and
Ladywood, and he never gave up on this dream all the years we
lived there.

1.

2.

1. Mom and Dad soon after they got married.

2. Mom at the back door of No. 29. NB tin bath right.

3.

3. Outside the Keyhoe's; our Joyce holds Bunny, Linda's arms are round two Humphries kids, with Kevin in front.

4. The dreaded mangle with Blackie the cat and Bunny the rabbit.

5. Me and the first Kevin outside the Nelson c1952.

4.

5.

At Home in Nelson Street

13

Everybody Needs ...

As dusk gathered in Nelson Street, the familiar shouts would bounce off the soot streaked, brick walls that enclosed our yard. It was always the same order.

"Patsy! Terry! Mary! Betty! Johnny! Archie!..... Gerrin!"

I knew what was going to happen because it always happened, winter and summer, rain or shine, and sometimes I ran up to our back bedroom window to get a better view.

The house next door was one of those that had been divided in two, and in the back part lived the Hunt family. In one room up, one down and an attic, lived Liza and Les Hunt, their six kids and two lodgers. One lodger slept on an ancient settee in their tiny living room cum kitchen, while the other slept in the attic, divided off from the kids' double bed by an army blanket strung on a clothes line. The Hunts were Irish Catholics, or 'duck eggs' as Dad always called them. We were surrounded by Irish families but Dad did not seem to like any of them much. Mind you, he did not like the Scots or the Welsh, and if there had been any black people around then, he would not have liked them either. My Dad was even handed in his prejudices.

Every night at about 9 o'clock, Les Hunt would stand at the kitchen door and call his kids in for bed. Always they were called in order of their age, with Archie, the eldest, coming last. A normal suburban scene this, you might think, but as each child - boys and girls alike, filed past their dad into the house, he would give them a sharp slap around the head. They knew what they were going to get and as they got near flinched in anticipation of the blow. This nightly ritual fascinated and mystified me, and I never got tired of watching. Was Les Hunt always in a bad mood at night? Was he belting them for something they might have done but which he had not yet found out about? Or was this the Irish way of showing who was boss in the house? I never managed to find out, but certainly, Les was not the boss, that was his wife Liza. What she said, or often screamed, went.

Because they lived next door to us, we had more to do with the Hunts in the years we lived in Nelson Street than with any other family. Liza was, I suppose, Mom's best friend, someone she could call on in a crisis, and there were many.

14

Although Dad was never openly hostile to the Hunts, and he and Mom often drank with Les and Liza in the Nelson, he let is be known that he would be most put out to find Liza sitting in our kitchen when he came home from work. In fact, his exact words were

"I don't want that fuckin' witch in 'ere when I come in fer me dinner."

Liza was always popping in to borrow something or other, or to tell Mom the latest gossip, or just sit and drink tea and complain about life in general. But Mom always had to make sure she had gone before Dad's return. Meal times were already dangerous enough.

But why was Dad so much against Liza Hunt? Well, for one thing he said that she was too foul mouthed. This was a laugh because everybody we knew swore all the time, including the kids. But there were unwritten rules about swearing. Us kids could swear at each other and at the other street kids, but never in front of Mom and Dad. This would merit a clout around the ear and a threat to 'wash yer mouth out with carbolic soap'. We could never swear at Mom and Dad, that would mean instant death, or at the very least, the 'belting of your life'. Mom and Dad swore all the time at each other, at us kids and at anyone else who happened to upset them, but in Dad's opinion anyway, Liza Hunt had taken swearing, well past the limits of normal, everyday obscenities. She had one particular favourite word that she used constantly, liberally sprinkling every sentence she uttered with this word in its past, present and future tenses. In fact, with her Irish accent it was often very difficult to make out exactly what she was saying, especially if she was in one of her 'paddys'.

One afternoon when Mom had kept me off school for some reason, we were sitting with Liza and Les in their tiny kitchen. Their kitchen always seemed to smell worse than ours. There were the familiar smells of cooking grease, urine and bleach, but there was also an overpowering stench of onions. I noticed this smell in a lot of the other Irish houses around, and even now the smell of onions brings back the sound of Irish accents and pictures of the Virgin sellotaped to peeling wallpaper. Anyway, on this particular afternoon, Liza was going on and on about some juicy bit of local gossip, but all I could really make out was the almost incessant variations on her favourite swear word. Les, who had been sitting quietly listening to this diatribe began to shift in his chair, then suddenly he stood up and flung his arms wide, as though about to conduct an orchestra. Liza stopped

15

talking and we all stared at Les in amazement. But still he stood there, arms outstretched, gazing as if in wonder around the now silent room. After what seemed like ages, Liza broke the silence.

"And what's a marrer wit you then?", forgetting to swear in her surprise. Les smiled down at her.
"Listen Liza, do you not hear it?"
"Hear fuckin' what?" she asked recovering herself.
"The quiet. And for a whole minute there I didn't hear the word "fuck", not even once. Wasn't it lovely now?" crooned Les. I suppose Liza's reply was inevitable.
"Fuck off." she snorted.

My Dad the Gaffer

In our street my Dad was a marked man. He was attempting to do what everybody around thought impossible. Alf Biddle was trying to make the giant leap from being a worker to becoming a gaffer. But everybody knew that gaffers did not live in two up and two downs in Ladywood. Gaffers lived in posh houses with gardens front and back, and gardens did not start until Edgbaston. For an ordinary working man with no capital living somewhere like Nelson Street to have ideas about starting his own business seemed to most people pure fantasy or the drink talking. But I soon found out that if my Dad said he would get something or do something, he always did, no matter how long and hard he might have to struggle. And it was a struggle.

He began by taking any metal working jobs he could get in any part of the country, leaving Mom to cope alone for days on end with the kids, the conditions and the ever looming bill collectors. For a long time he struggled alone doing everything himself, from getting work right through to the chasing up of bad payers, and there were plenty of them. When I was about 7 Dad rented a small broken down factory in Edward Street, just round the corner from where we lived, and he started to employ other workers. Even though Dad had only a couple of men working part time, to our neighbours, this confirmed it. Alf Biddle had made himself a gaffer, and as everybody knew, gaffers were rich. What our neighbours did not know was that on Fridays, Dad would often pay himself less than the men he employed. The men's wages always came first, then the factory rent, then money for Mom to feed, clothe us and pay bills until next pay day.

16

Us kids had no real idea of the hardships Mom and Dad had to suffer as he fought to hold on and build up the business. But working so close meant that Dad always came back for his dinner and was always on hand to be called out if a crisis came up at home. They often did. Even if he managed to get through his working day without interruption from Mom or one of the kids, trouble would usually be waiting for him when he came in for his evening meal. How many times I saw the "magic fork" swing into action I can't remember, but it is hard to think of Dad getting though any meal without an explosion.

For once it had been a quiet day, and Joyce, Linda, Kevin and me were playing quietly in the kitchen. Us kids had to keep quiet if we happened to be in the house when Dad was eating his meal. We had eaten our tea hours ago when we came home from school. For us it was usually a jam sandwich or, if we were lucky, a banana piece.[ie sandwich] Cooked teas were for workers only. Dad was sitting at the table with the *Evening Dispatch* propped against the teapot so that he could see what was on at the local picture houses. Mom took the dinner plate from on top of a simmering saucepan and placed it in front of him. Dad removed the covering plate and sniffed.

"What's this Nance, a bit of steak is it?" Dad knew very well what it was, but seemed in an unusually good mood and wanting to make polite conversation.

"Yeah, frazzled up ter nothin' it 'as. I'll tell that bloody butcher in the mornin'.", Mom said looking over Dad's shoulder. "Looks all right ter me.....", Dad said as he covered his meat and potatoes with thick, onion gravy from the big white jug. He added the salt and pepper, a blob of Colman's mustard on the meat and a slice of bread and margarine folded and propped ready against the rim of his plate.

As he picked up his fork, the kitchen door opened and round it appeared the bullet head of Terry Hunt. Terry was the second youngest from next door and by no means the brightest lad in the block. His concentrated stare forced Dad to put down his fork and ask,

"What is it yer want son?"
"Dad ses can 'e borrer the chopper please?" asked Terry in a quiet voice.
"'Course 'e can; pass it to 'im gell, will ya?"

I got up and found the chopper by the cellar door where we sometimes used it to break up big lumps of coal. I was about to hand it to Terry when Dad asked,

"What's 'e want it fer, any road?"
"'E wants ter chop Archie with it", Terry replied without a flicker of a grin.
We all stared at Terry. Dad glanced across at Mom, then back to Terry.
"'E wants ter do what with it?"
"'E wants ter chop Archie with it", Terry repeated without changing his grave expression.

Archie Hunt was the eldest son and always seemed to be in trouble for something or other, but he usually got a clip round the ear, not a blow from our chopper. It must be really something bad this time, I thought. Dad rolled his eyes to heaven and got up.

"Oh no, look, tell 'im we've lost it." He took the chopper from me and put it out of sight behind the cellar door. Terry still stood staring. "Tell yer Dad it's got lost, all right." Dad spoke louder now and Terry seemed to get the message, his head disappearing back around the door. Dad sat down again. "Fuckin' chopper. What next?" We did not have long to wait to find out.

Dad was at last managing to shovel down a few forkfuls of his meal when we all became aware of a rhythmic thumping sound from somewhere outside our kitchen door. We tried to ignore it but it got louder … and louder. Dad dropped his fork with a clatter.

"Oh fer fucks sake. Goo up and see what that bleedin' row is, will ya gell?"

I ran up to our back bedroom that overlooked the yard. It was getting dark and at first I could see nothing, but the thumping sound went on. Then, as my eyes got used to the gloom, I made out the familiar figure of Les Hunt on the far side of the fence. It looked just as though he was bashing a large and heavy sack of something up against our boards - thump, thump, thump it went. Then, as he pulled back the sack for an extra violent bash I saw that it was not a sack at all, it was Archie Hunt. Les was bashing his son's head repeatedly against our fence with a thump, thump, thump. I raced downstairs.

"Quick Dad, it's Les Hunt an' he's killin' Archie up against our boards." Dad ignored me and carried on eating determinedly. "Oh Alf, you'll 'ave ter do summat, that poor lad..." Mom started to get up but Dad slammed down his fork. "All right, all right. I'll sort it fuckin' out..." He stopped at the door. "You lot stay 'ere." he warned. For a few more endless moments the rhythmic sound of Archie's head against our fence continued, then silence.

We strained our ears but only the sound of muffled speech reached us. Then suddenly, loud and cheerful voices echoed around the yard.

"Good night Alf, see yer in the mornin'."
"Yeah, good night Les, see yer tomorrer."
"Good night Alf, all the best mate."

The Hunt's back door slammed shut and Dad came back in. The look on his face warned against asking any questions. He sat down and recovered his fork. What had Archie been up to? What had Dad said or done? We never found out.

"Fuckin' duck eggs.", was his only comment.

A Birthday and a New Arrival

'In our family we've got an heirloom,
It was handed to me just a year ago,
It's been in our possession since Grandad was a lad,
Now I'll tell you what it is and then you'll know.'

I often used to sing along to the George Formby song that Mom and me played on the old gramophone as we cleaned the best room. I would often strum my barometer ukulele, causing Mom to throw down her duster and collapse with laughter into the armchair. Of course, I had no idea what an heirloom might be, it sounded to me like something to do with bagpipes. But we evidently did have an heirloom in our family, not 'Grandad''s flannelette night shirt' as in the song, but something that had certainly been around when my Grandad was a lad. It was an ancient wickerwork crib in which my Grandad and his brothers and sisters had slept as babies, Mom and her brothers and sisters had used it, as had Tony, Joyce, Linda and me. With each new arrival the old crib was dragged out, dusted off and given a new coat of paint in the appropriate colour, blue or pink. In between times neighbours borrowed it for their new arrivals, and I often wondered just how many coats of paint that old crib had on it and how many sleeping babies it had sheltered.

In the weeks before my 7th birthday I noticed that Mom's belly was swollen again, and knew from experience that there would soon be another baby in the house. Her belly had been swollen just before my sisters had arrived, and now I saw the old crib being brought up from the cellar and put ready by the side of Mom's bed. I had been too young when Joyce and Linda were born to remember much about it, but now, going on 7 years old, I took my full part in the proceedings.

One morning Mom did not get up as usual, but stayed in bed after Dad had gone to work and sent me to fetch Liza Hunt. Then I was sent to the doctor's with a note for the midwife, whatever that was. When I got back Mom called me upstairs and told me to get Joyce and Linda ready to go out. When they were ready, Mom gave me a shilling [5p] and said,

"Tek yer sisters out fer the day somewhere, an' don't come back 'till teatime".

So, armed with a 3 penny [1.25p] bag of broken biscuits from the local shop, we set off for one of our favourite play places. With Linda in the pushchair and Joyce hanging on to the handles, we made for the City centre and Chamberlain Square. Changing into swimming costumes in the public lavatory outside the old Reference Library, we could not wait to start splashing about under those fierce jets of white water that gushed noisily into the basin of the fountain. For us kids, the fountain under the monument to Joseph Chamberlain was paradise. We could spend all day in the water, sit on the benches to eat our bis-cuits and feed the ever hungry pigeons with the crumbs. And there was the added excitement of searching the murky water for pennies and halfpennies thrown in for luck. Sometimes we would find enough for an ice cream or penny ice lolly from the cart. On a fine day, I was sure to see some of my friends from school and other kids from the streets around Ladywood.

The fountain made up for our lack of gardens or open spaces to play, and trips to the seaside. A day under those foaming, pounding jets made up for a lot. No one seemed to mind, no one ever moved us on or told us to clear off. The kids around the fountain today seem afraid even to put their hands in the water, let alone paddle. Maybe they know too much for their own good. We would run and jump, dive and swim until our skins were wrinkled and waterlogged and we were shivering from the cold, but not a thought of catching anything. I promised myself that I would not say this, but those really were the days. Well, some of them anyway.

When the Museum clock struck 4.00 and with our broken biscuits all gone, I decided that it was near enough teatime to start back home. Not bothering to change, we slipped our clothes on over wet costumes, there would be too much going on at home for any-body to notice. We ran down Newhall Street to keep warm, with Linda clinging to the sides of her pushchair and screaming in fear and excitement as I let it freewheel. Back in Ladywood at number 29, we found it was Liza Hunt who had cut our jam sandwiches, Mom was still in bed. Afterwards we crept upstairs to see the new arrival. This time the old crib would need a colour change as Mom had given birth to a bouncing, blonde baby boy, a second son, much to Dad's delight.

The the new baby was called Kevin, and in the excitement of his birth all thoughts of my impending 7th birthday had been pushed into the background. But now, with Kevin safely here, I started to drop heavy hints about what I wanted as a present.

In the little newsagent's shop just along the Parade I had seen a skipping rope. It had shiny wooden handles, a white rope with red flecks running all through it and cost 2 shillings and 6 pence [12.5p]. That may not seem very much, but in our house it was always a close thing to make the money last from one pay day to the next. Even with the usual help from the local pawnshop and 'strap' from the grocers, money often ran out. Nothing could be taken for granted, not even birthday cards and presents.

Although we all usually got something on our big day, there was always that uncertain feeling. But that skipping rope had become vitally important to me. Most of my friends at school had their own shop bought ropes, and my best friend Veronica had a super dooper model with even bigger handles than the one I had seen. I was still managing with a piece of Mom's old clothes line with loops for handles, and the other girls never let me forget it.

"Hey Carole, that ain't no skippin' rope, that's yer Mom's clothes line."
"What yer done with the washin' then?"
"She's gorra tek it back to hang her Dad's underpants on it."

21

If you thought little boys could be cruel they are just amateurs compared to little girls. To make matters worse, I had confidently told some of my mates that I would be having a brand new shop bought rope for my birthday, but all Mom would say in answer to my heavy hints was,

"You'll just 'ave ter wait an' see, wunt ya?" Now I wasn't so confident.

I woke up extra early on the morning of my birthday feeling hopeful. Leaving Joyce and Linda to sleep on, I went into Mom's room, took Kevin out of his crib and changed his nappy. This would be sure to put Mom in a good mood, I thought. Being the eldest girl, and with my sisters still being babies, Mom had given me the job of 'seeing to' Kevin whenever I was at home or off school. Before I was 7 I could change him, feed him, bath and dress him and look after him all day if necessary. But he was what they called a 'good babby', he did not scream or cry too much and always had a smile for me. In the main I enjoyed being his surrogate mom.

Downstairs, Mom was scraping toast over the sink and paid no attention to me when I came into the kitchen. Propped up against the tea pot was a large white envelope with 'Carole' printed on it in Mom's spidery hand. I tore it open and found it was the expected birthday card from Mom, Dad and the kids. I was pleased to see that she had remembered to add Kevin's name to the list of well wishers. On the card was a picture of a little girl about my age dressed in a raincoat and wearing wellington boots. She was sheltering from the rain under a red umbrella which bore the words 'You Are Seven Today'. As if I didn't know. As I ate my toast and drank my tea I kept glancing round the room for any mysterious parcels or lumps under tea cloths, but there were none and my heart sank. I drained my tea cup and pulled on my coat, but as I got to the door Mom called me back.

"There's summat fer ya in the front. Summat fer ya birthday."

My spirits soared as I ran into the best room and saw on the old piano, a small parcel. The paper was the brown greaseproof sort used for bacon sandwiches; Mom was never one for frills. I weighed it in my trembling hand, it was light enough, could it really be? Slowly I unravelled the thick paper and there it was, the skipping rope, polished handles, red flecks and all. I caressed the shiny handles and held the rope to my nose. It smelt fresh and new. I ran back into the kitchen to thank Mom and give her a kiss. She brushed me aside, but not unkindly.

22

"Oh goo on, you'll be late fer school if yer don't get a move on."

She was right, and with the rope clutched firmly in my hand,
I ran the 30 or so yards to the school playground. There were
dozens of kids all shouting, screaming, running and playing,
but I wanted all my friends to see that I had not been lying;
that I really had a new skipping rope. I would no longer be
'clothes line Carole'. I sought out an open space and began to
skip, doing all the fancy tricks I had learned with my clothes
line. Cross hands, double speed, then cross hands and double
speed backwards. After a few moments I realised that it was very
quiet; too quiet. I stopped and looked around, and to my horror
saw that all the other kids were lining up and ready to march
into class. In my excitement, I had not heard the teacher's
whistle. Mrs Davies, was staring straight at me.

"Carole Biddle, are you deaf? come here at once." I bundled up
my rope and ran to her, but as I got near I could see that she
was holding out her hand.

It had started to spit with rain as I trudged back home for my
dinner. Ignoring the curious glances of Joyce and Linda who were
playing in the yard, I crept into the kitchen and slumped down in
the armchair by the fire. Mom was clattering pots around on the
stove but she noticed.

"What's a marrer with you then?" she asked without turning.
"Nothin' Mom". (Sniff). She turned to face me. "Oh yes there
is... where's yer rope?" Got it in one. I started to cry.
"M. M. M. Mrs Davies ... t..t.took it off me ....'c..c..c..
cause I was skippin' after the w.. w.. w.. whistle ... an' she
ses I can't 'ave it b. b. b. back 'till next t.t.term."

I was expecting no sympathy from Mom, and probably a clout
round the head for losing my present so soon, but I was wrong.

"Oh she did, did she? We'll soon fuckin' see about that."
"She wunt let yer 'ave it Mom, she ses...", but Mom wasn't listening, she'd already gone.

I dashed into the front room and through the window I could see
Mom, hair in metal rollers and wearing her floral pinnie and pink
fluffy slippers, marching in through the school gates, her arms
folded determinedly across her chest. She vanished into the building and I wondered with some apprehension what was happening
in there. Mrs Davies had been very firm when she had said I could
not have the rope back until next term, but then again, Mom could
be quite firm too.

After a few moments I saw her come marching out again and, wonder of wonders, the rope was clutched firmly in her hand. She marched back into the kitchen and slammed the rope down on the table.

"'Ere, an' don't tek it there agin." She turned back to the stove.
"No Mom, thanks Mom." I gasped and ran out into the yard to skip until dinner was ready. The sun was shining again.

Friday Night Friends

Friday night was traditionally pay night, but for us it was also pay out night. After tea there would be a series of knocks on our back kitchen door. First the milkman, then the man from Blundell's who sold furniture on the weekly, then the Provident Clothing Supply man and the man from the Britannic Assurance Company to collect the payment on Dad's life policy. Mom would always pay this without fail and sometimes, when they had words, she would say,

"You're worth more ter me dead than alive Alf Biddle, ya bugger."

The next Friday night friend would usually be Taffy the tallyman. We had known him the longest of all the debt collectors, and I think he must have been Welsh because he 'talked funny'. Taffy worked out of a big warehouse along the Parade, and usually Mom had items of clothing from him, paying a few shillings a week off the bill. If money was particularly short one week, it was usually Taffy who was given the miss. One Friday when the familiar knock came at the door, Mom whispered to me,

"I can't pay Taffy this week. You goo an' tell 'im that I'm out".
I went to the door but without thinking said,
"Sorry Taffy, but Mom ses she's out." Taffy looked at me quizzically.
"Well, if she ses she's out, then she must be in, see?" But I did not see and just blurted out,
"She'll pay ya two weeks next week", and slammed the door.
Mom, who had been hiding behind it, slapped me round the ear,
"Now 'e knows I'm in, you prat."

The next caller would be our only female debtor. She was a tall, thin Jewish lady we all knew as Fanny and she wore steel rimmed spectacles with a stern expression. Fanny owned a millinery shop in Monument Road and she was a familiar figure in Lady-wood on Friday nights, pedalling around on her old bicycle to collect payments in a leather satchel slung over her shoulder. Again, Mom would pay two or three shillings a week 'off the card'. Everybody hated those Friday night debt collectors but we all needed them, and I suppose they needed us, but there was no love lost. When the story went round the district that Fanny had been knocked off her bike and the money satchel pinched, it cheered us up no end. When the last of the credit-ors had departed, Dad would often say,

"Ya wanna pay off that lot and don't 'have another fuckin' thing, or they'll bleed ya dry."

But it was not that easy. By the time Mom had paid the Friday night callers she would be short of food money for the coming week, so we would struggle through on credit, or strap as it was called, from our local shops. Gerry Marshall, the grocer, was always good for a cash loan of £2 or £3 until the next pay day. And so the cycle went on, strap, knock, loans, then the Friday night reckoning and round again. Everybody we knew lived like this, but it was Dad who realised that the only way out was to do it himself, build up his sheet metal business until we could get out of an environment where most people stayed in debt all their lives. But even when Dad's business did start to prosper, he always left paying bills until the very last moment.

Rob Dogs, Good Dogs and Other Shopping Problems

Mom was under the impression that all the local shopkeepers and tradesmen had entered into a conspiracy to rob, cheat and short change her at every opportunity. According to her they were all either 'crafty buggers' or 'bleedin' rob dogs', and the goods they palmed off on her were either seconds or 'shop rotten'. But des-pite these convictions she still had to patronise our local corner shops, for if we wanted to use bigger stores with a wider choice of goods it meant a tram trip up to the City centre to Lewis's, Greys or the Beehive in Albert Street. Even these well known stores found no favour with Mom. 'Huh, they can see ya comin' there, they can.' Which meant she thought them too pricey even to consider most of the time. But the main reason that Mom used our local family run shops was because of the strap.

Today, it is hard to remember how we managed in the days before supermarkets, hypermarkets and all night corner shops, but manage we did. From the time I was about 5 years old it was one of my little jobs to make a couple of trips a day to our local shops for food and other necessities. Mom would wrap the money in a note for the shopkeeper and, in summer, stuff it into the pocket on the leg of my navy blue knickers. In winter she would shove it down inside my glove and always issue the same warning, 'Now think what yer doin' an' don't lose me change or I'll tan yer arse.' So, carrying a folded brown paper bag and our ration book, I would set off along Nelson Street.

My usual destination was Gerry Marshall's grocery shop on the corner of Nelson Street and Summer Hill. It was a typical corner shop of the day, with a flapping red and white striped blind hung low over the front window. Bolted to the adjacent brick wall were metal signs that told us to buy Quink Ink if we wanted to write a 'Better Letter', or to 'Drinka Pinta Milka Day', and the one that showed Stanley Matthews telling us how much he enjoyed Craven "A" cigarettes. But my favourite was the one with a young man and his girlfriend grinning inanely at each other outside a shop. He was asking if she wanted an ice cream and she was replying 'Yes please, but it must be a Walls'. What drips they looked I thought, him with plastered down hair and her wearing that silly little pill box hat. When I grew up I would never wear a hat like that or complain about the make of ice cream my boyfriend bought me.

When I pushed open the door of that shop, a bell jangled and a host of interesting smells rushed out. Coffee beans, fire lighters, cheese and bacon were the strongest, and the sound of the big red bacon slicer whining through sides of meat was always in the background. Gerry Marshall was a jolly fat man with horn rimmed glasses and short white jacket. He was always very friendly to his many women customers, too friendly some husbands thought. But the shop was extremely popular, not just because of the man himself but because of the strap. If money ran out during the week, which it often did, Mom could send me down to Gerry's with a note asking that it be put on the bill. Gerry would note it down in his little black book for payment on the following Friday.

To anybody who did not pay on the due day, Gerry Marshall's friendly manner would vanish instantly and you would be likely to find your name and address and the amount owed on a post card in his front window. This usually did the trick, and there were few cards that stayed up for long.

There was another advantage to Mom shopping at Gerry's.
Sometimes when she had paid off the strap bill on a Friday,
and all the other bills, she would find herself short of cash
to last through the coming week. Gerry Marshall would lend
Mom £3 or even £4 in cash until the next pay day. Dad did
not know about this and would have gone up the wall if he had;
I was under threat of death never to mention it in front of him.
As you can appreciate, it was near impossible for Mom and lots
of the other women ever to clear their bills with Gerry, and of
course, this is what he wanted. He never added anything to the
strap bill or charged interest on the loans, but when I brought
Mom the sheet of notepaper with the list of items she had bought
over the week, she would sit down and check carefully through it.

"That Gerry Marshall's a crafty bugger." she would say running
her finger down the list for the third time. "I never 'ad two lots
of bacon did I? An' I never 'ad no biscuits this week, I know
that fer a fuckin' fact."

But she always paid up despite her misgivings about the bill,
for to fall out with Gerry would mean no more strap and no
more cash loans; things that in those days she could not do
without. Actually, the extra biscuits were probably added by
me, because I sometimes got a bag of broken ones for the kids
when Mom had told us to, 'Clear off, the lorra ya. An' don't
come back 'till fuckin' tea time.' I knew the routine.

"Mom ses can yer put 'em on the bill please Gerry?" It was a
gamble, but if there were chocolate ones amongst them, well
worth the risk.

Besides being on Mom's ever growing list of crafty buggers,
Gerry Marshall seemed to fancy himself as a pretty smooth
operator, a bit of a wide boy, as some people said. Mom would
say ''E never misses a bleedin' trick that one.' Once, when Dad
had a small win on Vernon's Football Pools, it did not take long
for the story to spread along the street. I can't remember now,
maybe we did exaggerate the size of Dad's win a bit, but by the
time the news reached Gerry Marshall's shop the amount must
have been quite substantial. One night after tea I answered a
knock at our front door to find no one there, but on the step
was a full crate of Mason's cream soda. Attached to the crate
was a note from Gerry Marshall congratulating Dad on his
good fortune and hoping that he, Gerry, would be able to
'serve you in the future as I have in the past'. Dad stared
at the note and then the penny dropped.

"The cheeky bugger, e's 'eard about me pools win. 'E wants me ter spend it round 'is bleedin' shop, the prat." Dad saw the funny side, as his win had only been 7 shillings and 6 pence. [37.5p]. It was a rare thing to be able to get one up on a local shopkeeper, so we enjoyed the pop all the more.

"Please Mister Hickman can I 'ave some cabbage leaves off the floor for me rabbit's dinner please?" The tall thin figure of the greengrocer looked down at me from behind a wall of orange coloured Ffyfes banana boxes,

"'Course you can love, an' there's some rotten fruit 'ere you can 'ave as well, if you like".

I liked, so Mister Hickman passed me down a large brown paper bag covered in wet stains. Hickman's was our local greengrocer and flower shop and another on Mom's extensive list of crafty buggers, but he seemed nice enough to me. I could not wait to get home and show Mom my haul of cabbage leaves and soft fruit. She looked into the bag and said,

"'Ere some of this is too good fer the bleedin' rabbit, you an' the kids can 'ave it after yer tea". She took the potato knife and carefully cut out all the bad parts from the apples, pears and bananas. After our tea we sat out in the yard and ate the lot, enjoying it all the more because it was free.

The next day I was back in the greengrocers for Mom's potatoes and Mister Hickman asked,

"How did your rabbit like 'is dinner then?"

I proudly told him what Mom had done and how we had eaten the fruit for our pudding. Mister Hickman smiled, but as I left there was a faraway look in his eyes. A few days later I went back hoping for more fruit, but this time there were only cabbage leaves. Outside was a large box marked 'Spec fruit, Six pence a Bag' [2.5p]. Mister Hickman had carefully cut out all the bad parts and put them back on sale. A crafty bugger or what?

Sometimes, as a special treat on Friday nights, Mom would send me to the top end of Nelson Street to Fazackerley's fish and chip shop. There were always long queues on Fridays, but I never minded waiting because I passed the time watching Mr Fazackerley working the chip machine. This was of grey metal and had a long handle sticking up on top. A freshly peeled potato was held on a small grill and the handle pulled to bring down a cutter which forced the potato through the grill, giving perfectly shaped chips. I was fascinated by how late Mr Fazackerley left it before taking his hand off the potato.

The chips would fall into a white enamel bucket, and when it was full he would tip them into the pan of boiling fat with a deafening sizzle. Then he would pull the shiny metal shutter across the spitting pan, moving it back occasionally to stir the chips with his wire mesh scoop. When they were cooked and served up, and the salt and vinegar hit the scalding chips, the smell was out of this world. The portions of chips were 4 pence and 6 pence [1.6p and 2.5p] and were wrapped in one sheet of thin white paper with and two sheets of old newspaper which Mrs Fazackerley would buy over the counter for 2 pence a bundle.

There was a long, scrubbed wooden bench running the length of the shop where we could sit and wait impatiently for the chips to cook. But woe betide any kid who put his dirty shoe on Mrs Fazackerley's spotless bench. When she was in a good mood or it was a big order, Mrs Fazackerley would throw in a portion of scratchings, or the crispy bits of overcooked fish batter that we all loved. In about 1957 Fazackerley's moved their shop to Icknield Port Road and we stopped going there. Later, we heard that Mister Fazackerley lost two of his fingers in an accident with the chipping machine and with them his interest in the business. With my child's morbid curiosity I wondered who had gone into that white bucket to sort the chips from the fingers.

Next door to the fish shop was Rogers pork shop. Not surprisingly, they sold home killed pork, bacon, sausages, pigs' trotters and tripe. Their home made pork pies were a legend in the district, and on Friday nights they outdid themselves with their faggots and peas. I would sometimes fetch these in a white pudding basin covered by a tea towel. Mister Rogers used an extra large ladle to scoop the faggots and thick brown onion gravy from the tall metal bin into the line of basins along the counter. Then a big scoop of bright green, mushy peas was plonked on top. It might seem strange now, but if you wanted chips with your faggots and peas you had to go next door to Fazackerley's. I would defy anybody to walk along Nelson Street on Friday nights and pass where the smells of chips and vinegar and home made faggots mingled and met, without feeling that they had not eaten for a week.

I never minded one bit going up to the faggot or chip shops because there was always something to interest me besides anticipation of the feast to come. But if I ever did get bored, there was always the problem of the dog to think about. Just across the road, almost opposite these two shops, there lived an old man who owned a black and white collie dog. The old man could hardly walk, so he often sent the dog out to do his shopping. It seemed perfectly reasonable to me that the dog should help out when times were hard, but there was one thing that baffled me. Every morning the dog would trot along Nelson Street to the newsagents in the Parade, with a leather wallet in his mouth, and come back with the old man's pipe tobacco and morning paper. On alternate Friday nights the dog, carrying a plastic shopping bag holding an envelope and money, would go across to the chip shop and bring back the old man's supper. On the Friday in between, the dog would carry a wicker basket with a white basin plus the envelope and money, and would queue in Rogers' for faggots and peas. That dog even knew his rightful place in the queue, and if any kid tried to get past him, he would send them back with sharp growl. Nobody pushed in front of that dog. I stood behind it many times and watched him trot home with chips or faggots and correct change in the envelope, and I tried to imagine the scene in the house. The old man carefully dividing the meal in half while the dog looked up at him with adoring eyes and barked his thanks. Well, I had seen quite a lot of Lassie films.

What bothered me all those months, or possibly years, was how did the dog know where to go on which day? I knew that Lassie could do it, but that was on the pictures and this was real life. The dog did not know what day it was, nor could it read the shop signs. It would be no use the old man just telling it where to go. Dogs, in my experience, were stupid, never did anything you told them and understood nothing. I saw that in our Rex every day. So how did he know, paper shop in the mornings, chip and faggot shop on alternate Fridays? The problem seemed insoluble and I had almost given up thinking about it, when one Friday night I was walking up to Fazackerley's. Twenty yards away the smells wafted over me, chips and faggots, lovely. Then suddenly I knew, it was the smell. Of course; the wallet smelt of tobacco, the plastic bag of chips and the basket smelt of faggots. That was it. I felt really pleased with myself as I queued behind the dog that night; he was not so clever as I had thought. But as he trotted away with the old man's chips and the white envelope, another problem flashed into my mind. How did that dog know it was getting the right change?

There was another local chip shop that we sometimes used, but my interest in it was not, for a change, the food. This shop was in Icknield Street and everybody called it 'the film star fish shop'. It was run by a Mr and Mrs Pretty who came from Handsworth, and they had a daughter called Violet who had gone to acting school in Birmingham. This in itself was unusual for that time and place, but what made it all the more thrilling to me was that Violet eventually made it to America and Hollywood, and become a true star of the silver screen. Her stage name was Anne Heywood and her parents shop was full of pictures of her and posters and stills from the films that she had starred in.

Although their chips were not as nice as Fazackerley's, I loved to stand in the shop of someone whose daughter was a film star. I would try to imagine her serving behind the counter, scooping pickled onions out of the big glass jar or shouting,

"Two cod an' chips an" a portion of scratchin's please." to her Dad standing at the fryer, but I could not see it.

But when one of Anne Heywood's films came to our local Lyric Picture Playhouse, I would stand for ages looking at the stills outside and marvelling at how a girl from out streets could be right up there, rubbing shoulders with the likes of Flash Gordon and Old Mother Riley and all my other favourites. To me, it proved that dreams could sometimes come true, even for people like us.

Veronica

I met Veronica on my first day at Nelson Street Junior School when we were both 5 years old. Even then I realised that she was somehow different from me and most of the other kids in the school. For a start, she always turned up looking very neat and clean, no holes in her socks, no tell tale stitching under the arms of her dresses, and Veronica wore 'proper' shop-bought ribbon in her long, dark hair. Not for her the cut up strips of rags that me and the other girls had to put up with. And Veronica brought cup cakes for her morning break and never cold toast like the rest of us. These were small, sticky pastries in paper pleated cups with a glazed cherry on top. I had never seen their like, and when she was in a good mood Veronica would swap a cup cake for a piece of my cold toast. I thought it odd that she enjoyed that as much as I did her cakes. Veronica's surname was Gibbs, so I called her Gibbs SR after the toothpaste. From that very first day until I left the district in the 1960s, Veronica was my best friend.

Veronica lived at the top end of Nelson Street, beyond the little island with its scraggy tree, at the posh end as we all knew it to be. She lived in a house similar to ours but in much better repair, with her parents and grown up brother whose name was Cedric. We all thought Veronica was a posh name and so was Cedric, and to me her home seemed posh as well. It smelled different from ours, or rather, it did not smell at all. No bleach, no grease, no urine and no screaming babies. As Veronica's brother was nearly 18 and already at work, this made her virtually an only child, something very rare around our way.

Veronica's home life was totally different from mine. No shouting, no swearing and no drunken punch ups on Saturday nights, but this difference seemed to fascinate both of us. Veronica's dad was a short, fat man with glasses who never seemed to say a word to anybody, least of all Veronica. Her mom worked as a bus conductress, a clippie as they were called. Again, it was unusual for the woman of the house to go out to work as well as her husband. I can't remember seeing Veronica's mom dressed in anything but her clippie uniform of a black jacket with silver buttons, black trousers and black, flat heeled shoes. She always carried a black tin box with a tiny handle, and I was always curious to know just what she kept inside.

One morning when I had got up early enough to call for Veronica on my way to school, she let me have a quick peep into the mysterious tin box while her mom was upstairs polishing her buttons or something. There was the familiar ticket rack with the different coloured tickets held in place by steel springs, just, like one of our mousetraps. Fourpennys (1.5p), sevenpennys (3p) and the workman's sixpenny specials (2.5p) for use only before 9 o'clock in the morning. There was her official Birmingham Corporation Transport badge with her number, lots of little brown paper bags for coins, dozens of elastic bands to seal them, and her leather satchel. With them was a packet of sandwiches, twenty Craven "A" cigarettes and some England's Glory matches. Our exploration had to stop as we heard Mrs Gibbs pounding down the stairs, but the one thing that I had really wanted to see was not there. I assumed that she must collect her shiny metal ticket punching machine when she arrived at the garage, so I did not get the chance I had always wanted, to press the little lever and ping a hole through the numbers along the edge of a ticket.

Sometimes after school, Veronica would take me home to play in her yard until her tea was ready. Being a virtual only child she was never short of toys, but her Mom would rarely allow her to take them outside the house. I would pester Veronica and threaten to go home and not be her friend anymore until finally she would run inside.

"Mom can I tek some of me dolls out to play in the yard, please?" she would always have to ask.
"Who are you takin' them out to then?" Mrs Gibbs would always want to know.
"It's Carole Biddle, Mom."
"Y'mean little Carole, with the blonde hair?"
"Yes Mom, little Carole."
"That's all right then… but don't you go away Veronica, your tea will be ready in a minit."

Veronica would run upstairs and fetch two or three of the big dressed dolls that were usually kept locked in her bedroom ward-robe. I would gape at them in wonder while Veronica watched me with some satisfaction. I hardly dared to even touch them with my grubby fingers, there were so new and clean. How any girl could be lucky enough to own just one of these dolls, let alone three or four, was beyond me.

Veronica liked coming to play in our yard, but with my list of chores building up I had little time for games. Mom would be shuffling pans around on the stove and trying to keep an eye on what the babies, Joyce and Linda, were doing, while I peeled potatoes in the sink or rinsed out dirty nappies in a bucket of bleach. Veronica would sit on our step peering around the door, taking in everything with her big dark eyes. If the smells from our kitchen revolted her she gave no sign. Mom also seemed to feel that Veronica was somehow different.

"Is that that Veronica Gibbs yer've got out there with ya?" she would ask without turning around from the stove.
"Yes Mom, she's playin' til her Mom gets 'ome from werk."

Mom would then make a snorting noise down her nose and carry on what she was doing without further comment. Was it Veronica she disapproved of or just women who worked? She never said.

Veronica would sometimes call for me on Saturday mornings to go to the ice rink or Monument Road swimming baths. Her mother provided pocket money for such trips, but I had to earn mine.

First I would clean our house, empty the slop buckets, lay the fire and run the errands. I was not paid for this and did not expect to be, but then I was free to clean two of our neighbours' houses, Molly Lunden and Peggy Keyhoe's, for which they each paid me 6 pence [2.5p]. Veronica would follow me from house to house, sitting on the step outside and watching everything I did with grave interest.

"Why do you do all this?" she once asked me.
"'Cause I fuckin' 'ave to." I told her, exasperated by the question.

Years later Veronica told me she once went home after watching me one Saturday morning and asked her mother if she could clean their house.

"Whatever d'you want to do that for?" Mrs Gibbs had asked in amazement.
"'Cause Carole Biddle does, Mom" Veronica had told her.
"Ah, well they've got too many kids, that's why she 'as to; you don't." came the reply and I suppose she was right.

So there it was, I envied Veronica her lifestyle, but in some way she seemed to envy mine. They were certainly very different although we lived in the same street, and probably this difference was the fascination.

At school other kids seemed to resent Veronica being different. She was a bit too clean and tidy with a bit too much pocket money to spend, and as for those cup cakes, well. To kids of that age, different is dangerous, and they either keep well away or take the mickey. So when it came to cookery, games or trips out, I was the only one willing to be Veronica's partner. I did not mind a bit, I liked her because she was different.

Kevin

I have a torn and faded black and white photograph of me, aged
about 8, holding our Kevin in my arms outside the Nelson pub.
On the window ledge behind is a half empty pint glass, which
must have been parked there by Dad while he took the photo.
It might have been taken on one of those Sunday mornings when,
with the dinner preparations well underway, I had taken Kevin
down to the pub to wait for Mom and Dad to come out. Kevin
looks just as I remember him, chubby, blonde and cheerful. He
was a 'good babby'; everybody said so. When he was born my
sisters, Joyce and Linda, were still babies themselves, so as
eldest girl and going on 7 it naturally became my job to look
after Kevin. There was nothing unusual in this, all the eldest
girls of all the families I knew had to look after their younger
brothers and sisters. No one thought it wrong or even odd, and
some girls just a couple of years older than me had five or six
kids to look after.

Kevin was a healthy baby until he was about 12 months old,
when he caught a cold that seemed never to go away. Eventually
Mom became worried enough to take him to our doctor's surgery
in St Vincent Street, where Doctor Dyson prescribed some med-
icine and some strong smelling ointment to rub on his chest. But
Kevin did not seem to get any better. He did not cry much, he
never had, but his breathing was odd and he had long coughing
fits that left him red faced and sweating, even in the freezing
weather of that November. Kevin slept in the blue painted wicker
crib at the side of Mom and Dad's bed, and because our house was
always very damp and cold in winter, I would put him to bed fully
clothed and wrapped up in a blanket as Mom had told me. One
morning I heard Mom telling Liza Hunt that Kevin had suffered
convulsions during the night and she would have to take him to
the doctor again. I had no idea what convulsions meant but I
guessed it was bad for our Kevin certainly was not his usual self.

On this particular evening Mom put Kevin to bed herself, dressing
him in a knitted yellow cardigan with leggings to match, a woolly
hat and little yellow mittens. She wrapped him in an old blue
blanket and put him into the crib, which she covered with another
blanket because it was a very cold night. Before they set off for
the Nelson, Dad called me into the kitchen.

"Now look, I want yer ter goo up an' look at yer bruvver 'bout every 'arf hour an' see 'e's all right. Will ya do that?"
"Yes Dad" I agreed, mystified at this sudden concern about Kevin. He had been all right all those other times I had looked after him, hadn't he? And what was I supposed to do if he wasn't all right I wondered.

Not long after Mom and Dad went out I got Joyce and Linda to bed without too much argument, did the washing up and sat in front of the kitchen fire. It was still only 8 o'clock. Tony was at his mate's house and would not be back for hours, so I began to doze. I woke with a start and looked at the clock. It was a quarter to 9 and I ran upstairs to check on Kevin. He was not asleep and his breathing was still noisy, but he managed a little smile when he saw me looking down at him. But it was so cold in that room I made sure that he had not pulled off his gloves and was still well wrapped in the blanket. Downstairs, I finished cleaning up the kitchen, made myself a cup of tea, then it was time to look at Kevin again.

As soon as I went into that freezing bedroom I knew something was very wrong. I stood in the doorway, my smoking breath visible in the light from the landing, and listened. It was very quiet, as if the room was empty. I crept towards the crib and peered down. Kevin's face was just visible among the folds of the blankets, but this time he did not smile up at me, he just stared with those big blue eyes. I reached down and touched his cheek, it was ice cold. Kneeling by the crib not knowing what to do, I looked at Kevin staring at me and waited for him to smile, or cry, or even blink, but he didn't. I knelt there for I do not know how long, until I began to tremble with fear or cold. The cold. Yes, that was it, I told myself. Get him downstairs in front of the kitchen fire, then he would be all right. But when I tried to lift Kevin from the crib his little body, usually so soft and warm, felt hard and cold, just like my big plaster doll. This frightened me even more and I dropped Kevin back onto his blankets and ran from the room.

I ran down the stairs and out of the house, heading towards the din of singing voices and a piano thumping out a popular song. I had never been inside the Nelson pub before, so I pushed open the first door I came to. The hot stench of tobacco smoke and stale beer hit me and people turned to see where the cold air was coming from. I saw Mom and Dad sitting in the far corner at the same instant that they saw me. Dad came over and bent down to my level so that I could smell his beery breath.

"What's a marrer gell?" he asked.
"It's our Kevin Dad, there's summat wrung wi'im." I whispered.

It might have been the look on my face, but Dad did not wait to hear any more. He ran out of the pub and back along the street towards home. Mom came over and took me by the hand, almost as if she had been expecting me.

When we reached the warmth of our kitchen, Dad had brought Kevin down and was holding him in his arms in front of the fire. There was an odd expression on his face but he said nothing. Mom went over and took Kevin. Seating herself in the armchair, she pulled the blanket away and looked into the baby's face. He was very pale and still staring. Then Mom covered his head with the blanket and began to rock him back and forth as she held him to her and stared into the fire. Dad stood watching her for a moment then said,

"I'll goo up fer the doctor Nance".

Mom did not answer, she just went on rocking. I sat down at the table feeling relieved they were home and that the doctor was coming to see to Kevin, but I did not dare speak to Mom or ask what was wrong with him. I just wished that he would cry and I could get him his bottle as usual. In a few minutes Dad was back.

"Nobody fuckin' in. I've put a note under the door fer 'im". Mom did not seem to hear and Dad turned to me. "You goo up ter bed now gell, it'll be all right in the mornin', you see".

Thankfully I ran upstairs and climbed into bed between my two sleeping sisters, fully dressed against the freezing night. All I knew was that there was something wrong with Kevin, but Dad said it would be all right, and if he said so.I was soon asleep.

I woke up the next morning to find Dad standing over our bed still dressed in his suit from the night before.

"Get yer sisters up now gell an' tek 'em over ter school. There's a bit of toast for yer in the kitchen but don't any of ya come in the front, all right?"
"But Dad warrabout...?" He cut me short.
"Listen what I'm tellin' ya, don't come in the front room."

I got Joyce and Linda ready, and downstairs we found a plate of toast getting cold on the table. There seemed to be no one else

around and I wondered why Mom had taken Kevin into that
cold front room if he was so ill. Joyce and Linda asked me
a lot of questions which I ignored, and I dragged them over
to the school as soon as I could. I knew that I should go back
home, and when I went into the kitchen, I was relieved to find
Mom nursing Kevin in front of the fire. Mom did not say a word
to me so I opened the cupboard, took out Kevin's feeding bottle
and started to wash it under the cold tap. Just then Dad came in.

"Don't bother with that gell, an' don't bother with school today.
You stay at 'ome and 'elp yer Mom".

Not long after this there was a knock at our front door and when
Dad answered it, I recognised the deep voice of Doctor Dyson.
They came through into the kitchen where the doctor put his bag
and black trilby hat on the table. He looked at Mom who had
not even noticed him come in, then questioningly at Dad. Dad
nodded and the doctor went over to Mom and tried to take Kevin
from her. For the first time, she looked up at him but would not
let go of the bundle. Doctor Dyson pulled the blanket back from
Kevin's face and looked closely at him. His face was very pale
and his eyes still wide open. The doctor poked the shiny instrum-
ent that hung round his neck in among the blankets and Kevin's
coat. After a few moments he came over to Dad and said quietly,

"I'm sorry Mister Biddle, but the baby's dead". Dad stared at
him.

"I could 'ave told ya that last fuckin' night at nine o'clock.
Where the fuck were ya.?"

The doctor did not answer but sat down at the table and began to
write in a small note book. As he did so I saw him take a quick
glance at his watch.

Dad came over to the top step of the cellar, where I had been
sitting behind the door, not wanting to hear what was said but
unable to avoid it.

"You goo up an' play in yer room fer a bit now gell."

Sitting on the bed upstairs, I tried to make sense of the past
twelve hours and what I had heard downstairs. The doctor had said
"the baby was dead", but he couldn't have meant our Kevin surely?
He was pale yes and quiet, but his eyes were still open. I knew

38

that dead people did not look like that, I had seen it often on the pictures. They got shot with bullets or arrows and fell down with their eyes closed, always closed, so how could our Kevin be dead? But I had an uneasy feeling. Why was Mom so unusually quiet? Why didn't Kevin cry for his bottle, and why wasn't it all going to be all right like my Dad had promised?

The sound of raised voices downstairs stopped these thoughts from racing around in my head. I could hear Mom screaming and crying, Dad trying to calm her, and over all that, the deep rumble of the doctor saying something about saving them some trouble 'at this sad time'. The front door slammed shut and I ran into the front bedroom. Through the window I saw Doctor Dyson place a small bundle on the back seat of his car and I recognised the old blue blanket that Kevin had been wrapped in.

A few days later some men came and put a small, polished wooden box with shiny handles in our front room, on top of the old gramophone. It was there for about three days. When I finally got courage enough to ask Mom about Kevin she told me, in quite a matter of fact way, that he had gone to live with the angels and we would not be seeing him again. But I heard some of the yard kids say the same as our doctor, that Kevin was 'dead'. This did not mean much to me at that time, and what had that little box in our front room to do with our Kevin? He could not be in there, surely? They would not do that to him. I had to ask Mom again and this time she told me that Kevin had gone to heaven. Well, I knew something about heaven from my Sunday school and they said that it was a very nice place to be, but you only went there when you were dead. So that must be the answer then. But where was this heaven, what would our Kevin be doing there all day, and how would he manage without me to look after him?

I hope I have not given the impression that Mom and Dad were, in any way, uncaring. I know that they were both deeply affected by Kevin's death, and I know Dad always blamed himself in some way. Looking back, I can now see that my Dad was the sort of man who never liked to show his true feelings about such things, but something that happened over two years after Kevin died showed me how deeply he had been moved.

It was a Saturday afternoon and Mom and Dad were back from the Nelson. They usually went for their afternoon nap, but this time Dad had stayed downstairs and seemed restless. I was just finishing the washing up when Dad turned to me and said those magic words that I never thought I would ever hear him say.

"Do ya wanna goo ter the pictures with me this afternoon?" I could hardly believe my ears as I had never gone anywhere with him on our own. Dad had never taken us kids to the pictures, he always left that to Mom. Joyce and Linda, who were playing in the yard, gaped at us as we passed them and went down the entry. They had never been anywhere with Dad on their own either. We strolled along the Parade towards the Lyric, and as we got near I could see that the film showing was called *The Jolson Story* and starred somebody called Larry Parkes. This meant nothing to me but I was delighted to find that it was a spectacular musical in Technicolor. I did not understand much of the story, but the singing and dancing were great and the idea of putting on black makeup to perform seemed brilliant.

Everything was all right until we got the part where Jolson kneels on a darkened stage, in a spotlight, and sings *Sonny Boy*. I glanced up at Dad and was shocked to see tears streaming down his face and falling onto his jacket lapels. I had never seen him cry and had never known him to get that upset about anything in real life, let alone something on the pictures. But as the song went on and I listened to the words, the penny dropped.

> 'Climb up on my knee Sonny Boy,
> Though your only three Sonny Boy,
> You've no way of knowing,
> And I've no way of showing,
> What you mean to me Sonny Boy...'

If Kevin had lived he would have been just 3 years old.

And when we got to the part about the angels taking Sonny Boy up to heaven, Dad picked me up and stumbled from the cinema. I know that Mom and Dad always did their best for us kids under difficult circumstances, but tragically, in our Kevin's case, their best had not been good enough.

Granny Graham's Garden of Rest

I never went to our Kevin's funeral because I had to stay at home and look after Joyce and Linda, who were too young to go. Mom and Dad took Tony, who was a couple of years older than me, but he did not tell me much except that Kevin was buried in Warstone Lane Cemetery. I could not understand that, because he was supposed to be in heaven with the angels like Mom and my Sunday school teacher had told me.

The Cemetery was not far away, so I went there and eventually found the little stone which bore Kevin's name, his date of birth and the date he died. I could not relate this stark slab to the cheerful, chubby baby that I had loved and looked after all his short life. But I found that the cemetery was a nice place to visit, away from the smells and noise of Nelson Street, it was just like being out in the country. There were a few scrubby trees, some blackberry bushes, patches of long grass and lots of dock leaves and dandelions. I would pick a few of these when I went to visit Kevin's grave so he would not feel left out, even though he was not really there.

I used to wander about trying to read the names on the other stones and picture how these people might have looked, walked and talked. How had they all come to end up in Warstone lane, I wondered? Were all of them really in heaven like our Kevin? From the size of the flower bouquets and elaborate decorations on some of the gravestones, I realised that the people who came to visit considered it a very important place. In my childish way, I too thought it was a good idea to have a garden where you could come to think about people who had gone to heaven.

The more that I thought about the cemetery, the more I liked the idea of it. I told Veronica all about Warstone Lane, but her mother would not let me take her to see it. Then one day she had a brilliant idea.

"Why don't we have our own cem'tree?" she asked. At first I did not understand what she meant. "You know, we could bury things that die there..."
"What things?" I wanted to know.
"Animals an' birds an' things... they don't go to heaven do they?"

41

I had to admit she was right. Animals and things certainly did
not go to heaven when they died. You could see them everywhere.
Dead dogs in the road, dead cats in the canal and sometimes dead
birds in our yard. I agreed that it was a brilliant idea.

"Yeah, we could find somewhere an' bury 'em and put their names
on an' when they got killed an' 'ow old they wus an' ...."
"But where can we do it?"

Veronica had put her finger on the one weak spot in our plan for
an animals' graveyard. Open land was very scarce around Nelson
Street, and Warstone Lane was too far away. None of the houses
we knew had gardens.... except for one. It was Veronica who
had another brainwave.

"Warrabout Granny Graham's then?"

Just around the corner up in Summer Hill lived an old lady that
us kids knew as Granny Graham. In reality she was Liza Hunt's
mother, and lived alone except for six Irish lodgers. At the
back of her house was a patch of stony ground where even the
weeds seemed reluctant to grow; the very place.

Granny Graham was busy frying bacon for her lodgers' breakfasts
when we turned up on her doorstep early the next morning. As
always, she smiled and seemed pleased to see us. When I tried to
explain what we wanted to do in her 'garden', she smiled again
and nodded cheerfully.

"Ah sure, you can dig out there if ya want to luv, it won't bother
me none fer sure."

Granny Graham was very deaf, so I do not know how much of
our plan she actually heard, but the important thing was, if it
came to trouble, I had asked. So far, so good, but who or what
was going to be the first occupant of our "cem'tree"? Although
we spent a long time looking, there was a shortage of animal or
bird corpses in Ladywood that week, so we had to think again.
Word had got round at school about our graveyard and one
night, a spikey haired lad from Garbett Street came down
our entry carrying a little paper bag.

"'Ere y'are, you can 'ave this for ya cem'tree." he said holding
out the bag. I took it from him and peeped inside. There was a
little green budgie, all stiff and cold. I gasped out my thanks
and ran up to Veronica's house clutching the bag. We were
in business.

We should have thought of it before. All us kids had pets of some sort and they were always getting run over or something, and then they would usually end up in the dustbin. Even a pet was entitled to a decent Christian burial; I knew that from my time at Sunday school.

Early one morning, so that we would not be seen by any of the other kids, Veronica and me made our way to Granny Graham's. From home I had borrowed a fork, half a candle found in the cellar and some matches. Veronica carried my Sunday School Bible and the little bag with the budgie. His name, the lad had told me, was Dandy, and he was about 10 years old. I dug a little hole with the fork and placed the paper bag gently on the bottom, piling the soil up over it. Then I stumbled through some verses from my Bible and we sang 'All Things Bright and Beautiful'. We could not keep the candle alight in the fresh breeze, but we scattered a few dandelion flowers over the mound as a finishing touch.

There was still something missing and we both knew what it was. Racing round to the newsagents in the Parade, we salvaged two wooden ice lolly sticks from the bin outside and raced back. We tied the sticks together in the form of a cross and, after much argument about the spelling, wrote on it in pencil, 'Dandee age 10'. We stood and looked in reverent silence at the mound and the little cross, satisfied that we had done all we could to give Dandy a decent burial, one that any pet could be proud of.

Word spread among the local kids, and soon Granny Graham's garden began to fill up with little mounds of former frogs, newts, a goldfish, a white rat and a grey mouse. So many kids brought their pets' corpses that we began to suspect that some of them had deliberately brought about their untimely end so they could witness the burial in our cemetery. Then the long summer holidays came and the graveyard business died off, if that is the right expression.

Having seen no new customers for about a week, Veronica and me set off on one of our favourite walks. We would scramble through the hole in the fence on St Vincent Street and stroll along the railway line, chatting about everything under the sun as the trains clattered past, only feet away. Of course, it was dangerous and we had been ordered not to go there by our parents, but that only made it all the more interesting. Even so, we never played any of the games we had seen some of the lads play, such as running across the track in front of a train to see who would be last or throwing stones up at the electric pylons to make sparks fly. Then there was putting pennies on the line to be crushed in half by the engine, or lying between the lines pretending they were going to let the train go over them, but they never did.

On that particular afternoon, we had not gone very far when Veronica stopped and pointed to a mound of earth and gravel by the side of the track.

"Ugh, what's that then?"

I followed her pointing finger and saw something black half buried in the soil. We looked closer and saw the head and front paws of a cat. The poor thing, we thought, it must have been hit by a train and it looked as though it had been there some time. We both decided there and then that this was no place for somebody's beloved pet to end its days, and that we would somehow get it back to our cemetery and do the right thing. Besides, we had never had anything as big as a cat; it would be a real challenge.

The trouble was that neither of us had the stomach to dig out the corpse. We did not know what we might find, maybe the cat's guts crawling with maggots, and we could not face that. But over the next week or two we both became obsessed by the problem of the dead cat. We went there every day to look at it and discuss the possible ways that we might dig it out and transport it back to Granny Graham's. We did not think it at all odd that every time we visited the dead cat it looked just the same and did not smell at all.

Then one morning, Veronica arrived at my house with a long pointed stick and another brilliant idea. We could use the stick to dig out the cat's body and then carry it on the end. In that way we would not have to get closer to the horror that might lie beneath it than about four feet. We spent all morning poking around the body with the stick, loosening the soil until we had uncovered most of its back and it looked as though we might be able to move it. The cat was bigger than we had thought, but screwing up our courage, we plunged the stick underneath the body and pulled. For a moment it stuck firm, but then it came away with a jerk and shot up in the air towards us. Screaming loudly, we dropped the stick and ran.

Looking back from a safe distance we saw that the cat had come free, but now looked very flat. Perhaps it had been run down by a steamroller, not a train. Cautiously we approached it again, nudging each other forward until we were within a couple of feet. No maggots, no bones and still no smell. Then we noticed that the cat had a little white square of cloth attached to its neck. Its name and address, we thought, and bent closer to read the words. We looked blankly at each other for a moment, then Veronica read the words aloud. 'Real fur nightdress case. Made in Hong Kong'.

We grinned sheepishly at each other. After that our 'cem'tree' seemed to lose its fascination and we were soon off in search of other adventures.

Did you ever see such a thing in your life?

Of all the critters that invaded and infested our little house, for sheer cheek and numbers the mice took the biscuit. Well, they did not actually take it, but chewed great holes in any left lying around. Among their other favourite targets were the blue paper sugar bags and the little grey boxes of gravy browning. When we opened the food cupboard on most mornnings, evidence of their nightly forages were scattered around with a fair sprinkling of droppings. The mice seemed able to get anywhere and every where despite the traps baited with stale cheese rind that Dad set every night. Most mornings there would be a couple of bodies lying in the traps, necks broken by the powerful spring, but this did little to deter them or reduce their numbers.

"I dunno where they all bleedin' come from..." Dad would say as he set another line of traps in likely places. "But I've gorra fuckin' good idea.", jerking his head towards the wall that separated us from the Hunts next door.

"Oh no Alf, they can't be. Liza's got more in 'ers than we 'ave in ours", Mom would remind him.
"Yeah, there's no more room for 'em there." Dad would mutter.

Wherever they came from, the mice were regular Houdinis at getting into and out of places that would have been near impossible, even for insects. One Sunday morning I got up extra early to do my chores and start the dinner preparations because later I wanted to go to Monument Road swimming baths.

45

After cleaning up the kitchen, laying the fire and filling the coal bucket, I opened the oven door and took out the meat tin. As usual there was a thick layer of fat from last Sunday's dinner. All families that we knew kept the meat fat from one weekend to the next because it would come in useful if food ran short during the week. The fat, or dripping, was delicious spread on thick fresh bread and covered in salt and pepper. But this time I saw that there were tiny marks running all across the white surface, like bird prints in the snow. Then I saw the familiar droppings and knew that our old enemies, the mice, had somehow managed to get into the oven, and out again. Along the line of footprints were larger holes where they had stopped to scoop up mouthfuls of fat. I took the tin and ran upstairs to show Mom.

"Look 'ere Mom, it's them bleedin' mice an' I gorra cook the meat in this." Mom's head came slowly from under the blankets, metal curlers hanging loosely around her face. She cast a bleary eye over the meat tin that I held out for inspection.

"Well, yer can fuckin' scrape it off, can't ya?" Brilliant. I might have known Mom would have the answer. Downstairs I took the bread knife and carefully removed the top layer of fat until the footprints and droppings were gone. I cooked our Sunday roast in that tin, everybody ate it and nobody got food poisoning. Lucky or what?

Not long after this there was an incident that convinced us we were probably fighting a losing battle against the mice. It was early November and preparations for Bonfire Night were well underway. All us kids looked forward to November 5th when we would have a massive blaze in the yard, with fireworks and home made goodies to eat. For weeks before the big night we would scour the district begging or stealing anything that would burn. Local factories gave us bags of sawdust and wood shavings, broken pallets and packing cases that we dragged home and piled high in the middle of the yard. Every night till bedtime, we would stand outside the Nelson with some old clothes stuffed with newspaper to make a vaguely human shape.

"Gorra penny fer the guy please mister?"
"What guy, where?"
"There 'e is, there against the wall, look."
"Bloody 'ell, the thing from outer space, more like."

But we usually got a good number of pennies and half pennies and these were saved up and spent at the newsagents in the Parade on Wilders or Brocks fireworks. They had names like Golden Rain or Silver Fountain, sparklers and Bingle matches. The boys went for Thunderflashes or Mighty Atoms and jumping jacks to throw at the girls.

It was this year that our Tony was going through his show business phase. He fancied himself as an entertainer and had constructed a near full sized puppet theatre from cardboard boxes begged from Gerry Marshall. He had spent hours with his water colour paint box covering the outside with intricate designs. The puppets were some of Tony's old socks, the holes serving as mouths, and for eyes he had glued on odd buttons. Tony's show was meant to keep the yard kids amused until the men got home from work and the bonfire was lit.

The puppet theatre was long and narrow and Tony had to pull it on like a tight fitting jumper, keeping his arms stretched out above him to reach the little stage. The show seemed to consist mainly of two socks fighting each other with pencils, but the dozen or so kids who sat watching did not mind and cheered loudly at every blow landed. It was this enthusiastic but unexpected response from his audience that must have caused Tony to get carried away. In the middle of a particularly manic sock fight he slipped and fell, the theatre still stuck firmly around him. This called up the biggest cheer of the night and the sight of Tony's legs sticking out of the bottom of the theatre and thrashing wildly as he struggled to free himself almost had his audience in hysterics. At last Mom was alerted by the noise and came out to drag him free by his ankles. This raised more cheers from the kids, who thought it was all part of the act. But Tony, red faced and cursing, could not see the funny side, and I thought it best to stay out of his way for the rest of the night.

To the first man home from work on November 5th fell the honour of lighting the yard bonfire. It was usually Dad, who could knock off early if he wanted. As he stuffed lighted newspaper into the heart of the pile and the flames began to grow, a rousing cheer echoed off the yard walls. It was Bonfire Night at last. One by one the other men in our yard would come home, have their meals and join their wives and kids watching the blaze. Sometimes they would make a night of it and send up to the outdoor for jugs of ale and ten Woodbines.

47

As the fire got going we would be driven back by the heat, and even the grimy yard walls would take on a cheerful orange tint. At the top end of the yard, old Ted and Lizzie who had lived there forever would drag chairs to their kitchen door and enjoy the spectacle and the heat. Golden Rain poured down onto the stone slabs, Mount Vesuvius erupted, illuminating the whole yard, rockets whooshed into the blackness, and Catherine wheels burned tracks on our fence as they whirled round on their nails. All night long there would be a procession of excited kids in and out of Mom's and Liza's kitchens for toffee apples, home made sweets and mugs of drinking chocolate, with faces and hands getting blacker and stickier as the evening wore on. Everywhere were the smells of burning rubbish, firework fumes and melted toffee.

On this particular Bonfire Night there was another attraction to come. The Hunts had recently bought a brand new settee 'on the knock' from Blundell's warehouse in Green Lane. This was an event in itself, because they had had the old one since anybody could remember and it had served as a bed for dozens of lodgers. Now the old settee was to be disposed of in the best possible way, on the bonfire. When the flames began to die down at last and the fireworks were gone, Dad and Les Hunt carried out the old settee and laid it carefully on the glowing embers.

We all stood around expectantly, and for a few moments nothing happened. Then we saw that the settee seemed to be moving. It was shaking, trembling, perhaps at the situation in which it now found itself. Then green and yellow flames began to shoot out and, as if on a given signal, the settee seemed to burst open and dozens of mice ran in all directions. The girls screamed and backed away and some of the women ran inside and shut their doors, but still the mice poured out of the blazing settee and ran for the dark corners of the yard. Two yard cats which had been sprawled out enjoying the heat were at first too shocked by the sheer number of mice to move, but now set off in frantic pursuit. Soon the mice were gone and the old settee just a black- ened lump, but their appearance seemed to have broken the spell of that Bonfire Night. The chill November air was closing in around us and it was time to go inside. As I followed Mom and Dad back to the light and warmth of the kitchen, I heard Dad say,

"Well Nance, now we know where them fuckin' mice are comin' from."

Always, after Bonfire Night had finished, I would kneel on the bed and stare out of the window at the remains of the fire until it faded into the blackness, or my eyes became too heavy to keep open. I was about to lie down when I saw a shadowy figure creep up the yard. It was Tony and he was carrying something. The fire suddenly sprang to life again, and I saw he was burning his puppet theatre, puppets and all. As Tony stood there in the fire-light, something I had heard on the pictures came into my head and it seemed to suit that moment. For a second I was tempted to open the window and shout it up the yard, but the thought of the clout round the ear that would quickly follow stopped me. I said it to myself without opening the window. 'Ah well, that's show business.'

Another Brother

Soon after baby Kevin died, Dad began to make changes to our house in Nelson Street. In his spare time between running the sheet metal business and working at night as a barman at the Nelson, he installed gas fires in all the rooms. He wanted no more freezing bedrooms. The council put in electric lighting and power points and life became a little more comfortable, especially in winter. Dad also fenced off our part of the yard and fitted a gate. He commandeered one of the lavatories and fitted his own lock so it would be for our use only. The key hung on a hook just inside the kitchen door. How many times, usually on a cold winter's night, did I trudge up to the lavatory block to find I had forgotten the key, then hurry back, swearing all the way.

I had no way of knowing at the time, but Mom and Dad must have been trying for another baby. Before they succeeded Mom suffered at least two miscarriages. One morning when she had stayed in bed and sent me to fetch Liza Hunt, I was alarmed to see Liza coming down our stairs with a bundle of blood stained sheets and the slop bucket full of what looked like blood. I was about 9 years old at that time and got the mad idea that Liza had murdered Mom. She handed me the gory bucket with the words,

"Carole, will ya go an' empty that for me, up the lavvy, there's a good girl".

I went, puzzled at how Liza could be so calm and matter of fact after doing the dirty deed. But I soon found out that all this had 'summat ter do with 'avin' babbies'. Betty Hunt told me, and as she was two years older than me, I thought she should know. It all happened again some months later when Liza handed me the sheets and the bucket.

"Empty this up the lavvy an' soak the sheets in it with some bleach when you've done it, there's a good girl."

This time I was not half so alarmed because I knew what it was all about. But I did wonder, if it was as Betty had said, why no new 'babby' had appeared in the house. Some time later I notic- ed that Mom's belly was swollen again, and when she told us kids that she would be going into Dudley Road hospital for a few days, I was certain. After a week Mom came home with a bouncing baby boy they named Kevin, and I was amazed and thrilled to find that he was the spitting image of the first Kevin. He was chubby and cheerful with wisps of blonde hair, another 'good babby' as it turned out.

After the birth Mom started to wear a stiff whalebone corset under her dress when they went anywhere special, such as trips to the pictures or away matches with the Nelson Ladies darts team. By all accounts, Mom was a very good darts player and in the pub had earned the nickname double-top. I had to help her struggle into the corset with a lot of wriggling and swearing, then help her out of it when she came back. Freed at last, she would stand in front of her dressing table mirror, slap the rolls of fat around her middle with the palm of her hand and say,

"Kids, that's what that is, fuckin' kids. Never again.", and that was how it turned out, the old wicker crib needed no more coats of paint.

I was soon back in the old routine of having days off school to look after the new Kevin, while Mom did the shopping, got the dinners and sometimes sloped off to the pub for a crafty 'half 'a shandy' with Liza. I had now passed my 10th birthday and thought I knew everything about our lives at number 29 Nelson Street, and with the episode of the blood stained sheets and bucket, had encountered all the horrors I was going to. But, like so many times before and since, I was wrong.

Getting home from school one dinner time, I found the kitchen empty. Pots were simmering on the stove, but there was no sign of Mom. I peeped into Kevin's pram but he was sleeping peacefully. Glancing up the yard I noticed that the door to 'our' lavatory was ajar. I walked quietly up to the block and saw the familiar red and white of Mom's floral pinnie inside the lavatory. She was holding an old stocking and there was something moving inside it. As I got closer I could see that the moving things were tiny, furry kittens, so young their eyes were not open. They were squeaking loudly as Mom plunged the stocking below the water and pulled the chain. She held it there for about a minute and when she pulled it out, there was no movement or sound. I was surprised but not as shocked as I would have been a few months before; I was fast becoming immune to such things.

"Mom, what d'ya do that for? It's cruel and we're s'posed ter be kind to animals, ain't we?" She turned to look at me without surprise or anger and said quietly,

"Yer gorra be cruel ter be kind."

I did not understand then, but I do now. In those days there were always unwanted litters about, mainly kittens and puppies. No one we knew could have afforded to have their animals neutered and litters put down humanely. It would certainly have been no kindness to let all the unwanted animals grow up to roam the streets, get run over or starve. Mom was right, it seemed cruel but was the kindest thing you could do because suffering was all the creatures had to look forward to.

But why did Mom take on this awful task? She had been the one too faint hearted to see my Bunny go in the pot when he got fat enough to feed us. When Dad raised a turkey for the Christmas dinner, it had been Mom who refused to touch the meal because the bird had become her pet. Neighbours often brought unwanted kittens and puppies for Mom to deal with in that way, and I think they gave her a couple of bob for the service. But the real reason she did it was that she had no patience with people who dithered when something needed to be done, to be tackled head on without excuses or get outs. And possibly she was proving to herself and Dad that she could do anything a man could do.

Because of what had happened to the first Kevin, Mom and Dad were understandably protective towards their new son. And because I looked after him most of the time, I had to be extra vigilant when it came to his well being. I was a lot older

51

now and would be able to deal with any emergency that might arise. At least that is what I told myself. As I have mentioned, our favourite summer play places were the fountains at Chamberlain Square in the city centre, but our second favourite was the back of Bingley Hall, especially at the end of the Ideal Homes Exhibition. All kinds of interesting 'stuff' would be thrown out or left lying around for anybody who cared to pick it up. This particular year we hit the jackpot and loaded Kevin's pram with long sheets of frosted glass, lots of shiny metal hooks and some rolls of green cloth.

With Linda hanging onto the pram handle and Joyce walking in front, we set off home with our booty. Everything was fine until we got to the top of Cambridge Street. I used to amuse Kevin, and sometimes frighten him, by pushing his pram a couple of yards in front of me, letting it freewheel and then hurrying after to grab the handle before Kevin started to scream too loud. This time the pram did not slow down. With the extra weight of our 'stuff' and the steep hill, it just kept on going. I had only taken a few steps towards it when I realised that I could never catch up.

It was heading down Cambridge Street towards the busy junction with St Vincent Street, King Edwards Road, Summer Hill and Nelson Street. Now, all the cars, vans, lorries and horse drawn vehicles in the city seemed to be converging on that junction from all directions. In that split second of terror, I realised that on its present course, the pram would pass the end of Edward Street, where Dad had his factory, and I had a vision of him walking home to his dinner as Kevin's pram shot past. I stared after the retreating pram and saw Kevin's expression of glee turn to fear. I knew that he would be crushed under the hooves of a British Rail carthorse or, the tyres of a massive BRS lorry. I could not move but I could still scream,

"Joyce! Joyce!"

My scream seemed to bring Joyce to life and she set off after the pram like a greyhound. I watched in an agony of suspense as Joyce slowly got nearer to the handle of the pram, and the pram quickly got nearer to the teeming junction. But as the front wheels reached the gutter, Joyce managed to grab the handle and dig her heels in. She and the pram skidded to a halt, the wheels suspended in the air over the road. Kevin was thankfully none the worse for his wild ride. Joyce had saved his life, I was sure of that, and in doing so, had probably saved mine as well.

1.

2.

3.

1. 'Ole Big Ead', Tony aged 10.

2. Veronica.

3. Our Kevin with Terry Hunt at the back door, c1955.

4. Outside number 29, Mom and Dad with me aged 11 and Kevin.

4.

Family and Friends

As we walked slowly along Nelson Street I made Joyce and Linda cross their hearts and hope to die on Christmas Eve if they ever told. They readily swore; if Mom and Dad found out what had happened we would all have got beltings. Perhaps there was something unlucky about the name Kevin, because he always seemed to be having narrow escapes. The runaway pram, hot rhubarb on his head one Sunday afternoon, holding his breath in the pictures, and I once had to pull him out of the River Severn at Stourport. But he survived all of this and more, so perhaps it was a lucky name after all.

Lost, Stolen or Strayed

At number 29 we were always short of money and living space, but we always seemed to have a good number of pets. Most of them did not cost us anything but were strays or other people's cast offs; dogs who had 'dirty habits', rabbits too aggressive to handle, cats that tore up everything in sight. I was about 10 when we had our largest menagerie. There was Rex, a cross bred Collie, Blackie, a stray cat, Bunny the rabbit, Joey the budgie, Nelson the goldfish and last, but to me certainly not least, Dicky Dick Dick the chicken. There were others who did not stay long enough to become family favourites, but I have fond memories of most of them.

Rex had long matted fur and was very smelly. Dad used to bath him in the Friday night bath water, after which he smelt even worse. Rex was a fire hog in winter and would lie as close as he could get to the coal fire in our kitchen until singing fur joined the other smells. When us kids came home from school, Rex would not leave his fireside position but lazily wagged his tail where he lay. It would waft in and out of the flames and often caught light. Rex would then dash behind the armchair in panic until one of us crawled in to beat out the flames. The thing I remember about Blackie, the cat, was that he managed to get himself stuck up the only tree for miles around.

Nelson the goldfish I had from Raggy Rowley, the ran and bone man, whose yard was in St Vincent Street. It was not until I had him home and tipped his plastic bag into Mom's pudding basin, that I noticed he had only one eye. Thinking of a name was no trouble. Sometimes when we got up in the mornings, Nelson would be floating upside down in his glass bowl on the kitchen window ledge. Mom would tip him into the sink, run the cold tap on him for a few moments and he would recover. Mom used to say

"Huh, he's only doin' it fer attention." I am almost sure that she was joking.

Bunny the rabbit had been given to us by a lady up the road who bred rabbits for eating, and he was supposed to be a sample of how tasty they were. But by the time he had grown fat enough to provide us with a decent meal, Bunny was our pet, and even Mom had not the heart to see him go in the pot.

Joey the budgie was our longest surviving pet and lived 19 years. He had been a present from Dad to Mom in their courting days and Mom had spent years trying to teach him to talk. Joey was what they call today a hard study, but Mom would not give up. For an hour or two almost every night she would sit under his cage repeating over and over again little phrases like

"Who's a pretty boy then?", "Joey loves Mommy" and "Happy Birthday Mommy". Some nights she would go on and on until Dad would explode,

"Oh fer christsake Nance, shurrup or gerrin' the fuckin' cage yerself."

At last Joey did manage to pick up two phrases. "Ta Ta Mommy" and "Pretty Joey". Then he would drive us all crazy repeating them over and over, until we had to cover the cage to shut him up.

Mom kept Joey's cage on a low sideboard in the kitchen. Blackie the cat always had his green eye on the main chance, and one day while Mom was pegging out washing he made his move. Jumping onto the sideboard, he knocked over the cage. So far so good, he must have thought. But our Rex in his usual fireside position saw what was happening and ran out to Mom, barking loudly. When she came in, Joey was pressed up against the bars on the far side of his cage while Blackie, had one paw through the bars straining to reach him. It was a scene from a Tweetie Pie and Sylvester cartoon, as Mom snatched up the broom and brought it down hard on Sylvester/Blackie's, back. Rex had saved the day and became Mom's favourite. Joey survived to say 'Ta Ta' to Mom for another few years, and Blackie never went near the cage or the yard broom again.

My favourite of all our pets was Dicky Dick Dick, the chicken.
How did I come to have a full grown chicken? Raggy Rowley
had been around as long as any of us kids could remember. He
was a small man who wore a long overcoat that touched the
ground and a flat check cap pulled well down over his eyes.
The sounds of his horse and cart trundling along Nelson Street
and his hoarse shouts of 'Rag, bone, iron', would send all the
kids running indoors in search of old clothes to exchange for a
balloon, or maybe a goldfish.

Most times when I ran in and asked Mom 'Got any old rags
Mom?', she would reply, 'Yes, I'm wearin' 'em', and that
would be the end of it. But on this particular occasion she
must have had a clear out or something, and I ran back with
quite a big bundle. I tugged Raggy's overcoat sleeves and he
took the rags from me and threw them onto his cart without
a second look. But this time there was no balloon or goldfish.
On the front of his cart was a large cardboard box full of fluffy
yellow chicks, all squeaking loudly, they could not have been
more than a few days old. Raggy dropped two of them into my
outstretched hands and trundled on. When Mom say my prize
she rolled her eyes to heaven,

"Oh God blimey, well, you'll 'ave ter look after 'em 'cause I
ain't."

I made them a home out of a shoe box and an old cardigan and
thought it wise to keep them down the cellar out of Dad's sight.
I was surprised when Tony found me an old table lamp with a
long flex which we plugged into a kitchen socket and ran down
to the cellar. I kept the lamp on night and day so the chicks
would not get cold, but thought it best not to mention this. For
a while, Tony's unusually helpful attitude puzzled me, until I
remembered, boiled eggs were his favourite tea, and he was
living in hope.

One of the chicks died a few days later, but the other grew and
prospered and eventually took his place with our other pets in
front of the kitchen fire. I named him Dicky Dick Dick but
for the life of me I can't remember why; I did not have a
stammer.

What I liked about Dicky was that he was not a fussy eater. He
would try anything, and I mean anything. His favourite was a bit
of my jam sandwiches, but he also liked dog food, cat food, the
rabbit's lettuce and the budgie's seed. I never tried him on fish

food but I am sure he would have approved. Dicky would always be waiting at the back yard gate when I came home from school, clucking round me and pecking at my hands anticipating treats to come. Then one afternoon I came down the entry and could not see him. He was not in the yard or even in front of the kitchen fire. I turned to Mom who was peeling potatoes at the sink.

"What's 'appened to Dickey, Mom?" Without turning she said, "He's in the dustbin". I thought she must be joking.
"Oh come on Mom, where is 'e?" She turned round to face me.
"Look, 'e gorra stone stuck in 'is throat an' 'e was chokin' an' ya Dad 'ad ter kill 'im. 'E put 'im in the bin up the yard."

I still could not believe her, but raced up to the line of dustbins outside the lavatory block. The first two held just rubbish and fire ashes, but in the third, almost covered by tea leaves and potato peelings, was my Dicky. His head was lying at a funny angle to his body and, when I poked him with my finger, he was cold and stiff. His usually bright and beady eyes were covered by a white film. Yes, he was dead all right, and it was my Dad who had killed him.

I tried to fathom out why Dad had done it. Not just out of spite surely? Perhaps he thought I loved that chicken more than him. True, Dicky never hit me, swore at me or told me what to do, but he was just a chicken and Dad was - well, Dad was Dad.

For days after I could not bring myself to speak to Dad or even look at him, and he made matters worse by not telling me just what had happened. But when I thought about Dicky, I remembered that he was always picking things up in the yard and trying to eat them. Bits of string, pieces of wire and yes, stones. He would usually cough them up with much squawking and wing flapping, but this time he must have bitten off more than he could swallow. It must have happened the way Mom had said, but why stick him in the dustbin? Even pets must be entitled to a decent burial, I had learned that much from Sunday School.

I soon got over Dicky's untimely death, and besides, sulking and moping only got you a clout round the ear in our house. Anyway, I still had Rex and Blackie and Bunny and Joey and Nelson, and then there were the renegade pets, those that did not stay the course for one reason or another. Like the big brown mongrel dog that Dad brought home one night.

It had been hanging around his factory for days and he had taken pity on it. For my Dad to do that the animal must have been a truly pathetic sight. He brought it on the Saturday but by Sunday dinnertime, we still had not decided on a name. The roast and veg that I had just finished cooking were on the table and we were all waiting expectantly in front of our empty plates while Dad was washing his hands at the sink. The dog with no name took one look at that pork joint, could not believe his luck, and before any of us could stop him, jumped on the table, snatched it up and was down and out of the back door in an instant.

We all shouted to Dad who set off down the entry in hot pursuit of the dog and our dinner. Us kids ran into the front room so that we could follow the chase through the window, but the dog turned left down Nelson Street and he and Dad were lost to sight as they headed for the Parade. After a few suspenseful minutes, we saw Dad coming slowly back along the street. He was empty handed, red faced, out of breath and out of temper. Obviously the dog had been able to run faster than Dad, even with our joint in his mouth. We were all thanking our lucky stars that it was Dad and not one of us who had brought home the nameless one.

Dad slammed the kitchen door shut behind him.

"Right, that's fuckin' it. No more fuckin' animals in this 'ouse, d'you 'ear?"
"Yes Dad", we all agreed meekly as we tucked into our dinner of potatoes and two veg.

Only a few days after the incident of the disappearing dinner I was sitting in the science class at school when the teacher, Mrs Stanley, made an announcement.

"I have a lovely little kitten, she needs a kind and loving home. Is there anyone here who would like a kitten?" Without a second thought I put my hand up.
"Have you got any other pets, Carole?"
"No miss" I lied. "Would it be all right with your parents?"
"Oh yes miss." I lied again.

After all, I reasoned, surely Dad's animal ban applied only to dogs. It had been a dog who had pinched the meat, not a harmless little kitten. Then Mrs Stanley wanted to bring the kitten over to the house one afternoon after school, but I could not risk this. I made an excuse about having to get things ready and she arranged to meet me on the next Saturday morning outside the Edgbaston Picture House.

On the Friday I plucked up the courage to mention the kitten to Mom, but she was not encouraging.

"Well, you'd better not bring it 'ere, you know what ya Dad said."

I knew only too well, but what possible objection could he have to an innocent little kitten? Perhaps when he saw it he would be charmed and let me keep it. I tried to imagine Dad being charmed and changing his mind, but I could not. All I kept seeing was his face when he had said 'No more fuckin' animals in 'ere.' Perhaps I could keep the kitten out of his sight for the rest of its life.

Saturday morning came and I hurried along to the Edgbaston cinema, excited at the prospect of a new pet but full of fore-bodings about its future. Mrs Stanley was there with the kitten in a proper cat basket and she had brought some tins of Kit E Kat to start me off. She made me promise to look after the kitten and I thanked her and plodded home with a heavy heart. When Mom saw the basket she rolled her eyes to heaven but said nothing. The kitten was a beautiful little bundle of white fur with four black feet, but when Joyce and Linda saw it all they could do was clap their hands on their mouths, point at me and say, almost in unison,

"Whoaaah, you wait 'til Dad gets 'ome."

I waited, playing with the kitten in the front room. At last I saw Dad's overalled figure go past the front window, heard Mom talking to him in the kitchen and I could guess what about. Dad came into the front room still wearing his black work beret. Once again, he had been called into action before his fork got anywhere near dinner. He was not in a good mood. He stood for a moment looking down at me and the gambolling kitten.

"What did I tell you lot the other day?"
"Don't know Dad", was all I could think of to say.
"Yes ya do. No more fuckin' animals in 'ere I said, didn't I?"
"Yes Dad", I agreed.

Dad took the kitten from me and went to the front door. For a terrible moment I thought that he might drown it in the drain outside, so I ran upstairs and peered out of the bedroom window. But all he did was put the kitten gently down on the pavement and shut the front door. The kitten stretched, looked around and walked off in the direction of the railway. I pressed my face against the window to watch its progress until my view was blurred by tears and the rain that had started to fall.

The kitten had gone but another nightmare started. Every day Mrs Stanley would ask me about the kitten. If it was eating well, if it was getting bigger? Had I started to house train it yet? And worst of all, what name had I chosen for it? I had to think fast, and somewhere at the back of my mind was a song that I had heard at the pictures - 'Felix kept on walking, kept on walking, kept on walking still'. So his name was Felix and the lies came thick and fast, so many and so convincing that I almost expected to see Felix waiting for me in the yard when I came home from school. I was terrified that Mrs Stanley might take it upon herself to cross Nelson Street and see Felix for herself, or ask me to bring him to school. What then? I would never be able to pass off our elderly and all black Blackie as Felix.

Eventually, like all incidents to which we attach such importance, the saga of the kitten passed into history. Even so, I felt guilty for a long time about what had happened to Felix. I had let that kitten down, I knew that, and often wondered what became of him. The direction that he had been heading along Nelson Street would have have taken him past the coal yard on the corner. They had a fierce Alsatian dog who used to stick his snarling muzzle under the double doors, hungry for blood. I hoped that my Felix had imitated his namesake and, 'kept on walking, kept on walking still'.

I was not the only one in our family with pet problems. Every night around tea time, Nelson Street would echo to the sound of Tony's voice shouting, 'Nigger, Nigger, Nigger.' He was calling in his all black mongrel dog for his tea; it is not a name you would use now. When Nigger had been just a pup, Tony had teased and tormented him unmercifully and he had grown up wild and excitable. Eventually we had to keep him in the yard tied to the handle of the brew house door. Nigger had also developed 'dirty habits' and was never allowed indoors.

One particular day I had been playing out in the street, jumping, off the loading bay of the factory opposite, when I had fallen and grazed my knee. I ran in to Mom for treatment and sympathy but got little of either.

"Dunno what ya mekin' all this fuss about, it's only a scratch."
I was sitting on the wooden draining board at the side of the sink and Mom was half heartedly dabbing at my knee with the dishcloth. I was about to jump down when a dark figure loomed up in the kitchen doorway. We turned to see that it was a police sergeant, and he was obviously out of sorts.

"Is that your dog outside, the black 'un?" he asked sternly. Mom went to the window but there was no Nigger in the yard and his rope was hanging loose. I realised that when running in with my cut knee I had left the gate open, and Nigger must have made a break for freedom, as he often did.

"I said, does it belong to you?" the policeman repeated irritably.
"Why, 'as it bin run over then?" Mom asked cautiously.
"No, but it's just fetched me off me bloody bike." He dusted the knee of his uniform trousers as if to prove the claim.
"Well I can't 'elp that can I? He's s'posed ter be locked in the yard, one of the kids must have left the gate open". Mom was equally unsympathetic to adult injuries. The sergeant stood for a moment staring at her then a thought occurred to him.
"'Ave you got a licence fer that dog, then?"
"Yes we 'ave." Mom replied, and continued to dab at my knee with the dish cloth. The sergeant obviously through he was on to something.
"Can I see it then - that's if ya don't mind."
"You'll 'ave ter wait, me daughters cut 'er leg an' I gotta see to that first", replied Mom without looking up from her task.

Suddenly, her unsympathetic attitude vanished and she set about dressing my knee with the thoroughness of Florence Nightingale. She produced a clean white towel, a bottle of Dettol, some cotton wool and something I had never seen in our house before, a box of Elastoplasts. The policeman sighed heavily, folded his arms, leaned against the door frame and looked critically around our kitchen. We both knew what he was thinking. 'They ain't got no licence for no dog, they ain't, never in the rain of pig's puddin', they ain't.'

At last Mom completed her surgery on my knee and turned to the sergeant.

"Now, let's see, what was it yer wanted?"
"Now look 'ere missus ..", the policeman began....
"Oh yeah, that's right, the dog licence."

Then Mom made an elaborate pantomime of searching. In the drawer, under the clock on the mantelpiece, even under the cushion on the armchair she hunted, but no licence appeared. The policeman was shuffling his boots impatiently when Mom seemed to think of something. She went to the dresser where she kept some of her best china and took down an oriental teapot with, 'A Present from Barmouth', inscribed in gold around the base. Lifting the lid, she took out a small roll of paper and handed it to the sergeant with a flourish.

He looked at it suspiciously, then unrolled it and inspected the contents. Holding it at arms length he inspected it again. He seemed disappointed.

"Yes, well that does seem to be in order" he muttered. Handing the licence back to Mom he turned to leave. "But keep that dog under control in future, it's bloody dangerous." Mom mouthed an eight letter word at his retreating back, and it was not farewell.

1. Kevin aged 7 with Linda, 9.

2. Christmas at the Keyhoe's c1955.
l to r - Peggy Hunt, Liza Hunt, Mrs Handwicke, Granny Graham, Dad (hidden), Mom (minus teeth), Peggy Keyhoe, (back row), Cornelius Keyhoe (knee level) and two other neighbours.

Sunday, Bloody Sunday

For me, Sunday was never a day of rest, it was usually the most
hectic day of the week, especially if I wanted to go swimming
at Monument Road baths before dinner. I had to be up extra
early, fetch the papers and take them up to Mom and Dad with
a cup of tea. Then I must empty the overflowing slop pail, get
Kevin up, wash, dress and feed him, and make sure that Joyce
and Linda were up and dressed. Next I had to clean the house,
lay the fire, peel the potatoes and shell the peas ready for
dinner. At last and only then, could I get away to the baths
for an hour or two to play at being Esther Williams.

I had to be back from the baths in time to see Mom and Dad
off for their dinner time visit to the Nelson. Then I would
start the cooking, keep one eye on the dinner, another on
the babby and also see that my two sisters did not get into too
much trouble. After dinner I washed up while Mom and Dad
went up for their afternoon nap. We all had to be dead quiet
during these hallowed hours, for to wake Dad up meant instant
death. I usually took our kids and some of the neighbours up to
Graham Street in the Jewellery Quarter, to the Sunday School
at Elim Pentecostal Church. We had to be back home in time
for me to wake Mom and Dad with a sandwich and tea, giving
them time to get ready for their evening session at the Nelson.
Then I needed to get the kids some tea and keep them occupied
until bed time, clean the house again and make sure everything
was tidy for when Mom and Dad rolled back at about 11 o'clock.

I was just 9 years old, and at this time we still had old Flossie
living with us. She was the last of my Gran's original lodgers
and slept in the attic room. She had been around as long as any
of us kids could remember, but we did not usually see much of
her. She kept 'herself to herself' as she would say, except for
Sundays when she had her dinner with us.

We all knew that there was something wrong with old Flossie.
Today they would probably call it senile dementia or something,
but then people said that she was a bit barmy. She liked a drink
and was very forgetful, especially when it came to paying her
rent, and she was always muttering to herself. We never understood what she was on about and could only pick out the odd
swear word. Dad had wanted to get rid of Flossie for a long
time, but Mom felt sorry for her.

"Oh Alf, we can't just put 'er out, where's she gonna goo?"
"Don't give a fuck where she goos as long as it ain't 'ere."

But Flossie kept out of Dad's way, and as long as she did that
he did not press the matter.

On this particular Sunday the dinner preparations had gone unusually well, with no panics, no disasters, not even a narrow
squeak. Nothing happened that would bring Dad's wrath down
on my head, or rather ear. With saucepans bubbling on away
on the stove, I would stand on our front step and watch for
Mom and Dad to come out of the pub. The smell of boiled
cabbage was everywhere, and the sounds of *Educating Archie*
or *The Billy Cotton Band Show* on the Light Programme could
be heard from a dozen front windows. As soon as I saw them
leave the pub, I would dodge back inside so that the plates
were already piled with roast potatoes and two veg as they
walked through the door. The meat would be on the big
turkey plate ready for Dad to carve.

This time I saw not two, but three, figures come out of the
Nelson. The third, shorter and shapeless one, I recognised
as old Flossie. Dad had been in an unusually good mood that
day and had even bought Flossie a couple of drinks, which
makes it even harder to understand what followed.

The kids and Tony came in from the yard and we took our
places at the table. Dad carved the meat and we passed round
the gravy jug, then the salt and pepper, with many pleases and
thank yous. Dad was always very strict about table manners. The
meal was roast beef and Yorkshire pudding, and as Dad's fork was
poised over his roast potatoes he realised something was missing.
He glanced around the table.

"Can you pass us the mustard Floss please?" Dad asked politely.
The pot of Colman's mustard was right in front of her but she
ignored the request. She just kept chuntering to herself and
jabbing her fork into her dinner in an aimless sort of way.
Tension mounted as Dad raised his voice.

"Floss, can ya pass us the mustard, it's just there in front of ya?"
For a moment she carried on muttering then looked Dad straight
in the eye and croaked,
"Gerrit ya fuckin' self."

Dad gaped at her, we all stopped eating and gaped at her. Then
Dad looked sharply at Mom as though he might have misheard.

"What the fuck did she say Nance?" Mom tried desperately to cover up.
"Nothin' Alf. Tek no notice, she's only ... "

Flossie might just have got away with swearing at Dad at his own table if she had had the sense to stay quiet. Mom could probably have smoothed it over. But to our horror Flossie repeated, only louder this time, those immortal words,

"Gerrit ya fuckin' self." The expected explosion was not long in coming.

Dad jumped up, grabbed the edge of the table with both hands and tipped the lot, dinners and all, over onto Flossie, or rather onto the spot where she had been only seconds before. Senile or not, Flossie had somehow scrambled out of the way. But the nightmare was only just starting. Even before our plates had stopped rolling around the floor, Dad had dragged Mom into the front room and locked the door behind them. As we stood snivelling in the remains of our Sunday dinner, we heard Mom and Dad screaming at each other. Dad was accusing her of taking Flossie's side against him and a lot more. Kevin was screaming in his high chair, bewildered by the sudden loss of his dinner and frightened by all the noise. I saw our Tony roll his eyes to heaven and head for the back door and his bike. He was away out of it and I could not blame him.

Suddenly we realised that the shouting had stopped and there was an ominous silence from the front room. Scared even more by this, we ran outside and peered in through the lace curtains. We could just make out two figures locked together, grappling over the back of the settee. Dad's hands were fixed tight around Mom's throat. No wonder she was not screaming.

Joyce and Linda burst out crying, and in a panic I ran next door and dragged Les Hunt away from his Sunday dinner to intervene. After a lot of door banging and shouting through the keyhole, they came out. There were Dad's red finger prints around Mom's neck and she had the makings of a black eye, but she was not badly hurt thank the Lord. I was glad I had been to Sunday school for the last few weeks, that might just have swung it.

Now we were all afraid that Dad might go in search of old Flossie, the cause of all the trouble. But in the excitement, she had packed a couple of carrier bags and slipped away, and we never saw her again. Dad was pleased about this and so was Tony, who claimed the attic as his bedroom, away from the bloody kids, as he put it.

Mom and Dad made it up in time for the evening session at the Nelson, but I heard later that Mom had not been slow to display her battle scars. That night she had made a point of asking neighbours,

"An' 'oo do ya think did this, then?" I could just imagine Mom angling her head so that the black eye caught the light. And when the neighbours were unable to guess the culprit, "'E did, 'im there, Alf bloody Biddle, yes, 'e did it.", jerking her head towards Dad as he waited at the bar. There was surprise all round at this revelation because Dad was never rowdy or violent in public, even when drunk.

Mom wore her bruises with something like pride, but to me it did not make any sense at all. How could two grown up people be killing each other one minute and lovey dovey the next? I had not yet heard about what they call a love hate relationship, but it was not to be too many years before I went through it myself.

Sunday was the day that Fate often chose to play her most vicious tricks on me. Feeling a bit bored I suppose, she would drop me in it, then watch with interest to see if I could get myself out. I usually did, but this only ensured that her next trick would be even worse. Fate played exactly the same game with Betty Hunt next door. Like me, she had the job of looking after the younger kids and getting the Sunday dinner while her Mom and Dad were drinking with mine at the Nelson.

On this particular Sunday we were dividing our time between watching our dinners cooking on their respective stoves, and skipping in the yard under the pretext of keeping our eyes on the kids. This arrangement worked well for a time, but then we got carried away with our skipping game and forgot the dinners. The minutes flew past pleasantly but then, almost simultaneously, we remembered.

We dashed back into our kitchens, but in my case Fate had already been there. The saucepan of soaked peas had boiled almost dry. Under the remaining peas was a thick layer of black slimy stuff. That's it, I thought, now I would get the 'belting of my life' when Mom and Dad came in. It was Betty's fault,

I told myself, she had made me play stupid games when I should have been watching the dinner. Now she would have to help me put things right. I ran next door with the pea pan where Betty was straining the hot water from a saucepan of potatoes. She was pouring it into the sink, down the narrow gap left by the ever present bowl of dirty nappies.

"Look 'ere Betty, me fuckin' peas 'as burned, what am I gonna do?" Betty turned to look, grinning broadly,
"Well, what the fuck can I do?" No sooner had she spoken than Fate provided an answer. Looking at me, she let slip the plate that had been holding the potatoes back in the horizontal saucepan, and the whole lot sploshed into the bowl of dirty nappies. Betty was mortified.
"Oh no. I'm gonna get the beltin' of me life when Mom comes in." In her panic she turned to me.

"It's your fault Carole, gooin on about ya fuckin' peas, now me taters is spoiled." She was almost in tears. I was tempted to say 'Well, what the fuck can I do about it.?' but Betty was right, I had distracted her at a crucial moment, and besides, if it came to it her belting would be far worse than mine.

I helped Betty pick the freshly cooked potatoes from the nappy bowl. Then we swilled them under the tap and sniffed. Ugh - bleach. It took lots more swills under the tap to get almost rid of that clinging stench. Now it was a race against time. Could we get everything back to normal before our parents rolled in from the Nelson? It was a close thing. With only minutes to go I left Betty with her soggy potatoes and ran back home to salvage what I could of the peas. I scraped the black slimy stuff off the bottom of the saucepan with one of Dad's old screwdrivers; it did not leave too many scratch marks. The surviving peas were a bit brown around the edges, but an extra thick gravy would mask that. When Mom and Dad came in they were in a good mood for a change, and the dinner was served and eaten without adverse comment. It was the same in Betty's house and no beltings were handed out that day. We had got away with it. As Mom and Dad clumped up the stairs for their afternoon nap, I marvelled at what a few pints of Ansell's mild ale could cover up.

Some Sundays Fate turned her unwelcome attentions from me to one of my sisters. Even so, I was the eldest and supposed to be in charge, so I was always caught in the crossfire. There was a threat that all of us kids lived under then, and it was the certainty that if you did (or did not do) a certain thing, you would get 'the beltin' of your life'. We all had beltings, and these were bad enough, but this other was the ultimate, the worst that could possibly happen and something to be avoided at all costs. It was on one rainy Sunday afternoon that our Linda found out what was meant by that ultimate belting, and I still say that it was all her own fault.

It began innocently enough. I was just starting the pile of washing up, Kevin was fast asleep in his pushchair and Joyce and Linda were starting their usual Sunday afternoon bout of arguing and fighting. Every few minutes I would turn from the sink and hiss,

"Shurrup you two, if ya wake Dad up we've fuckin' 'ad it."

It was no good, on and on they went getting louder and louder. I threatened them with the worst punishment that I could think of.

"If you two don't fuckin' shurrup I'll throw ya down the cellar." I knew that they were both afraid of the cellar because I had often told them about the giant spiders that lived there. But this time they came back at me with a cheeky reply and carried on carrying on.

"Right, that's fuckin' it." I told them. "C'mon, down the fuckin' cellar ya go." I grabbed Linda who was the lightest and smallest, and after a bit of a struggle got her to the cellar door, opened it and pushed her down the first few steps into the darkness. Then I slammed the door and latched it. As I began to struggle with Joyce, Linda started to scream and shout and bang on the cellar door. Joyce was bigger and heavier and put up a better fight than Linda, and it took me longer to get her to the door. With one arm round Joyce's neck, I slid back the latch, but as I did so, Linda shot out and ran past us into the yard, screaming in triumph.

"Yah Carole, can't get me down the fuckin' cellar, can't get me down the fuckin' cellar." Joyce and me looked at each other in alarm. We both knew things were getting well out of hand.

Then we heard it, the soft pad padding across the ceiling above our upturned faces. Our eyes dropped to stare at the stair door, transfixed, waiting for what we knew was about to happen. Outside, Linda was happily unaware that anything was wrong.

68

"Yah, Carole, can't get me down the fuckin' cellar, can't get me down the fuckin' cellar."

The stairs door flew open and there stood Dad. His face was red, his eyes were starting from his head and he was breathing heavily. He was wearing only his long sleeved interlock vest and underpants which came down below his knees, leaving a few inches of hairy leg above short, black socks. He looked much as Stanley Matthews might have done after a 3 - Nil defeat, but we did not laugh. Laughter was the furthest thing from our minds. Outside our Linda had finally gone quiet, probably sensing that all was not as it should be.

Dad marched over and slapped me hard across the face, bringing stinging tears to my eyes. Then Joyce got the same and he looked around for Linda.

"Where is she?" Dad growled, and we both dumbly pointed to the yard, holding the sides of our faces and snivelling quietly into our cardigan sleeves. Dad went outside, closing the door behind him and then we heard those terrible sounds. We could see nothing but we both knew that we were hearing our Linda getting the belting of her life. Slap followed slap and scream followed scream and it seemed to go on for ages. At last, Dad came back inside and, ignoring Joyce and me, went upstairs, his face even redder and breathing more heavily. Then, as Joyce and me stood trying to cry quietly, Linda came slowly back inside. We stared in awe at the livid handprints on her face as we all continued to sob into our cardigan sleeves. Even now I still had to have the last word.

"S..s..see, I...t..t..told ya w..what w..w..would a..a..'appen d..d..didn't I?" I did not cry for long though; I still had the washing up to do.

Thankfully, not all Sundays were so traumatic. We did have some quiet and peaceful ones; well, we must have done, but it is not hard for me to remember another Sunday when Fate allowed me to feel safe, then struck when I was least expecting it. This was the Sunday of Kevin and the Rhubarb. Dinner had passed off peacefully and Mom and Dad were snoozing upstairs. I had finished the pile of washing up and could now get out for a bit by taking the kids and myself off to Sunday school.

When I was about 4 years old, a kind lady had called at our house and asked Dad if he had any children. I can almost see

Dad's grim smile as he nodded. The kind lady was named Mrs Miles, and she volunteered to take Tony, Joyce and me to Sunday School each week and bring us all safety back home. This had been an offer Dad found too good to refuse, and from that day until I turned 15 I attended the Elim Tabernacle in Graham Street in the Jewellery Quarter.

When Linda was old enough, she came too but she and Joyce lost interest after a couple of years. Tony went only a few times, then stole 3 pence [1.25p] from the collection plate and felt too guilty to show his face again. But I stuck it out for several reasons. On that first afternoon Mrs Miles had shown us scenes from the Bible illustrated with coloured felt cut out figures stuck on a large board. I loved these and also the frequent slide and film shows. This was my first introduction to pictures both moving and still blown up on a big screen, and I suppose this is where my fascination with films started. Besides, there was always some lively hymn singing accompanied by Pastor Dyke on the piano.

"C'mon let's raise the roof.", he would bawl as he thumped the keys. When he shouted this I always glanced anxiously at the roof looking for signs of daylight. But the main reason I went to Sunday School all those years was that it was one of the few means of escaping from the chores, the rows and the ever watchful eyes of Mom and Dad. Even when I became a teenager they raised no objection to my going, though they both knew that the dreaded species called boys also attended. They probably thought that any boy who went to Sunday School could not be too bad and, in the main, they were right.

Graham Street was where I met my very first boyfriend of all. His name was Dermot O'Kelly and I think he was Irish. He was my boyfriend in the sense that I saw him there every week, but I made the mistake of telling Veronica about him. She insisted on joining to see what he was like, and after a few visits told me that she too had fallen in love with Dermot. By then though, I had gone off him, so that was all right. Next Veronica went the other way and decided to become a nun. When I reminded her of this recently, her only comment was, 'I wish I bloody had now'.

To get back to the rhubarb. Up to the time we came back from Sunday School the day had gone well, and I was preparing one of our favourite treats for the kid's tea - rhubarb and custard. It was raining outside so Joyce and Linda had to play in the kitchen. They began to get on my nerves, arguing and fighting and making almost enough noise to wake up Mom and Dad. Kevin was crawling around the floor looking for mischief to get into. I was at the stove simmering the two pans of rhubarb and custard and shushing the kids.

Fate took me unawares and to this day I do not know how it happened. I was stirring happily at the custard when Kevin suddenly grabbed my best Sunday skirt with his mucky hands. I looked down and pulled away, and the next thing I knew was that the rhubarb saucepan had tipped over and the hot slushy mess was pouring down on his little head. The clatter of the saucepan had stopped Joyce and Linda's fighting and they were staring at Kevin. I stared down at him in horror while a thousand thoughts raced through my head. What to do first? Grab Kevin, grab the saucepan, and what about the custard? My mind was made up for me when I saw Kevin slowly open his mouth to let out a yell of pain and indignation. If Dad woke up and came down I would be dead. If Kevin was hurt, I would be dead. Even if he survived, I would still be dead when Dad found out, as he surely must.

Before Kevin could release his first scream, I clamped my hand firmly over his mouth, picked him up and ran out into the yard. Still keeping his mouth clamped, I wiped away a layer of rhubarb and looked at him more closely. The rhubarb had not been as hot as I feared, thank the Lord. No, he was not burned and he was not going to be scarred for life. I talked quickly.

"Shh now Kev, you're all right bab, I'll get all this nasty stuff off, and then Carole will give ya some lovely custard, eh?" He began to calm down and I was able to release my hand from his mouth. "Would ya like some pop an' a biscuit? You can 'ave 'em all if you don't cry, bab." He seemed convinced and choked back his sobs.

Inside, Joyce and Linda looked at Kevin as though he had come back from the dead, but I screamed quietly at them to start cleaning up the kitchen. Then I salvaged as much rhubarb as I could from the saucepan, stove front and lino. I rubbed the remainder out of Kevin's hair with a wet towel as he munched his biscuits and drank his pop. Then I made Joyce and Linda cross their hearts and hope to die in a cellar full of rats if they ever told what had happened that afternoon.

Kevin was too young to swear an oath, but he seemed to have got over his rhubarb shower and Mom and Dad had slept on peacefully. Well, it had not been such a bad day after all, and soon Sunday would be over for another week. Now, if only Mom and Dad could be in a good mood when they came back from the pub later that night; but that was probably a hope too far. One prayer had been answered that day.

A Sixpenny Sick Note

Even though my school was just opposite our house in Nelson Street I was always late, dashing in through that rusty iron gate just as the teacher on playground duty blew the whistle. It grew worse when Joyce and Linda were old enough to go, because I had to make sure they were clean and tidy and had eaten their breakfast toast before dragging them across the street with me. I always wore one of Mom's old cardigans for school, and one winter morning the headmaster, Mr. Lubbock, came up to me in the playground.

"Carole Biddle, why aren't you wearing a coat?" he demanded. "Don't need one sir, I only live over there" I replied pointing across Nelson Street to number 29. "That doesn't matter, it's freezing. You wear a coat tomorrow," he ordered. I had not the heart to tell him I had no coat, so I kept out of his way for the next few days.

I was very proud when my class teacher, Mrs Osbourne, chose me as milk monitor. This meant that at break time I had to fetch the crate full of little bottles from the yard and hand them out to the other kids, along with drinking straws. One straw each but two for my friends. There were always a couple of bottles of milk over and Mrs Osbourne let me have them. No winter coat, rags for hair ribbon and always hungry, she must have felt sorry for me. As far as I remember, I enjoyed my school work and was getting along quite well until I was about 7 years old. This was when Mom started to keep me off school to help with the house-work, go shopping, look after my younger brother and sisters, or sometimes just for company. This is when I started to fall behind with my reading and writing, and I never caught up.

Sometimes when I was dusting and polishing our front room, I would look out of the window towards my classroom across the street and wonder what the other kids were doing. In my innocence I never minded a bit being kept off school, and as I scrubbed, mopped and swept my way around the house and yard, dressed in one of Mom's old pinnies, I felt really grown up. Most other girls I knew were also kept off school regularly by their hard pressed or, sometimes, just lazy mothers. We all had our younger brothers and sisters to look after on an almost full time basis. I had Joyce and Linda and later, the first and second Kevins, but other girls only a bit older had four or five kids from babes in arms to hefty toddlers. All this was thought normal where we lived and I do not remember ever hearing about kids being taken into care, or whatever they called it then. When I returned to school after odd days off, Mom would scribble a note for the teacher saying that I had been suffering from a sore throat or, if she felt really creative, that I had been 'bilious'.

If we were off school for three days or more in a week then we had to have a doctor's note. On the Friday night, when Dad got his pay, Mom would send me to Doctor Dyson's surgery at the top end of St Vincent Street to get a sick note for school the following Monday.

The surgery was a very old, dark building and the patients had to sit on a long, hard wooden bench waiting their turn in an almost bare little room. Doctor Dyson would never call out the next patient's name or even 'next please', but would just give a kind of grunting cough from behind the closed door. This meant go in, but it must have been very confusing for any new patients. He never examined us when we went for school sick notes, but took our word that we had a cold, or something similar. When I walked into the consulting room his hand was always poised over the sick note pad, but he would never put pencil to paper until he had asked that vital question, peering at me over the top of his glasses. 'Have you got your sixpence with you then?' [2.5p]

Doctor Dyson always charged us for a sick note, but there was another, younger, doctor that we called 'the nice one' and he never asked for our sixpences. Sometimes I would take a gamble and spend the sixpence Mom had given me on sweets as I walked up St Vincent Street. Once I bought a bundle of liquorice sticks to chew while I waited in the surgery. That night my gamble paid off because the nice one was on duty. He asked what had been wrong with me and I told him 'tummy trouble', as Mom had told me. He was about to write out my note when he suddenly looked up and asked me to put my tongue out. I did and for a moment he looked startled as it was completely black from chewing the liquorice. Then he smiled and said

"There's not much wrong with you, Carole Biddle."

Too many days off during a school term would being a visit from the 'School Board man'. He would ask lots of awkward questions and emphasise how important it was that every child take advantage of the free education generously provided by the City Council. The School board man was a regular caller in and around Nelson Street, but his pleas were lost on most of the mothers.

On any school day there would be a fair number of kids off. The School Board man would start at the top of the street and make his way down. But by the time he reached us the grape-vine would have done its work, and Mom would have sent me to bed so that she could tell him, at least half truthfully, that I was sick in bed. The danger was not always over then. The School Board man was on Mom's long list of crafty buggers because he had been known to walk around the block then come back down the same street. This way he hoped to catch kids who, minutes before had been too ill to get up, playing a full blooded game of football in the yard, or worse still, staggering back from the shop with a bag full of potatoes.

The more I was kept from school the further I fell behind with lessons and the less I wanted to go back. It was not long before most lessons were an acute embarrassment to me, except for drawing, painting and sewing. I know that I was just as much to blame as Mom for I never missed the chance to aid and abet her in my truancy. There were many dinner times when I would say,

"Mom, why don't you an' Liza goo ter the pitchers this after-noon? I'll look after our Kevin if ya keep me off." She would usually agree. I know that they would sometimes spend the afternoon in the Nelson while I got the kid's and Dad's tea ready. But pub or pictures, Mom was always back on duty at the stove when Dad came in from work.

Blind Eyes in Nelson Street

Old Ted and his wife Lizzie had lived at the top end of our yard since anybody could remember. Their one up, one down and an attic was the last in the block, right up against the yard wall and opposite the block of brick lavatories. To me and the other kids Ted and Lizzie seemed really ancient, from another age.

Lizzie always wore black; a long dress reaching down to the ground which was covered by an equally long coat, and black boots with buttons up the sides. She always wore the same battered black hat fixed by a piece of elastic under her chin, and fingerless woollen gloves in winter and summer. I never saw Ted dressed to go out, in fact I never saw him go outside that tiny house except on the hottest of summer days, when he would drag his old armchair to the doorway and sit dozing in the sun. He always wore baggy trousers with braces, a waist-coat that did not match and a collarless striped shirt. He had a few tufts of grey hair on his head and his skin was the same colour, with little blue veins all over his nose and cheeks.

Old Ted had something wrong with his legs. When we peered in through the grimy window we would always see him sitting and making his paper spills. He would roll them from sheets of old newspaper and sell them to neighbours as firelighters for a penny or two a bundle. Some Monday mornings Mom would send me up with our Sunday papers, and Ted would let me help him by tearing the sheets to the right size. In winter there would never be a fire in the grate, but they would wear their big coats or have blankets draped around them.

I do not think that Ted had any shoes because I never saw him wearing anything but a pair of old checked slippers, with the toes cut out to ease his corns. Despite their obvious poverty, Ted and Lizzie were a quiet and friendly couple who never caused any trouble or asked anything of anybody. Neigh-bours would often take them pans of hot soup or cast off clothing, or give them a few coppers for a jug of beer, but it would never have crossed anyone's mind to seek help for the old couple outside the yard. There was a strong distrust, even dislike, of officialdom, and most people went out of their way to avoid coming in contact with it except to pay their weekly rent. If only somebody had thought to ... but hindsight is a wonderful thing.

Lizzie would earn a few coppers from Mom and the neighbours by running errands, errands that Mom thought I was too stupid or too small to handle. Every Monday morning old Lizzie would put her head round our kitchen door and call in her croaky voice,

"Anythin' ter goo today Nance?"

Usually there was something to go. It would be a parcel with Dad's best suit, a couple of his good shirts and his Sunday shoes. They were 'going on their holidays' as Mom called it. Their holidays were taken in Icknield Street at the local pawnbroker's shop. Mom would get a loan of about 15 shillings [75p] for her bundle, and this would help see her through the week with the help of strap from the local shops. Most families we knew sent their Monday morning bundles with old Lizzie and she got 3 pence or 4 pence (1.25p or 1.6p) for her trouble. The next Saturday morning, Lizzie would bring back the bundles and Dad's best suit would be pressed in time for weekend visits to the Nelson and the Railway Club. Interest was due on all loans, and if you could not repay the loan and interest by the due date on the pawn ticket, then the goods would be sold in the shop.

It was one of those frequent Mondays when Mom kept me off school to help with the housework, or perhaps just for comp-any. Twelve o'clock came and went and we saw no sign of old Lizzie. Mom started to get anxious because she was depending on the pawnbroker's cash for that week. She went out into the yard and looked towards Ted and Lizzie's house. The dustmen were making their rounds, carrying the rubbish to the dustcart in rusty tin baths balanced on their heads. Two of them were bending and peering in through Lizzie's kitchen window. One of the men came down the yard towards us and as he got near we could smell on him the sour stench of kitchen waste.

"'Ere missus, we think there's summat wrung with old Ted. Will ya come an' 'ave a look?" Mom followed him up the yard and I tagged along behind. She joined the men at the tiny kitchen window and, shielding her eyes from the daylight, peered through the ragged lace curtain. I could not get near enough to see, but after a moment I heard Mom's voice.

"Oh my God." I knew it must be something bad as she did not even remember to order me back to the house before opening the kitchen door and going inside.

I stood at the door behind the bin men and peered into the
dark little room that was Ted and Lizzie's kitchen and living
room. After a few seconds I could just make out two seated
figures. There was Ted in his usual armchair in front of the
empty fire grate. He was not moving and his head was thrown
back, mouth gaping open. He looked as though he was staring
at the ceiling. Lizzie was sitting in a wooden chair near him,
holding a bowl and spoon. In the bowl was some white stuff
that looked like porridge. She was spooning it into Ted's open
mouth, but most of it seemed to have run down his chin onto
his crumpled waistcoat and trousers. Mom went over and laid
a hand gently on Lizzie's arm.

"What's a marrer Liz, what's 'appened then?" Old Lizzie turned
to look up at Mom, her face a wrinkled mask of bewilderment.

"'E wunt eat 'is dinner.", she croaked plaintively.

My blood ran cold as I heard those words, for I knew I was looking at a dead person. I stared at Old Ted's waxen face. His eyes
were open, just like our first Kevin's had been when the doctor
said he was dead, but I had not believed it. So that is what you
looked like when you died. Mom tried to take the dish away
from Lizzie but she would not let go, she just sat there staring
at Ted's upturned face. Mom sent me to fetch Liza Hunt and
somebody went for the doctor.

"Well 'e can't goo like that, can 'e?" Mom said, looking down
at Ted's food caked clothing. She sent me back home to fetch
one of Dad's second best shirts, then they closed the door on
me while they got Ted ready to be taken away.

It turned out that the old man had been dead for about five days.
All that time Lizzie had been feeding him, washing him, talking
to him and carrying on as though nothing had happened. No one
in the yard had missed either of them until Lizzie failed to
turn up for the Monday morning pawnshop bundles.

Mom had said, "Poor old cow... but she'll get over it in a bit".
But the poor old cow didn't. Every night, as soon as it got dark,
the harsh sound of old Lizzie's voice could be heard from the top
end of our yard. She was out there in all weathers, shouting,
screaming, cursing and shaking her fists at the sky, reviling God
for taking her Ted away. It went on for weeks and us kids were
too frightened to go up to the lavatory block after dark in case
we bumped into her. Some of the older lads did venture up but
soon came running back when Lizzie started her performance.

"She's fuckin' mad.", Archie Hunt had told me and my sisters one night. "An' she's gorra knife." He made a lunging motion towards us and we screamed and ran indoors.

Then one day, Lizzie was not there any more and the house was boarded up. In the corner of the yard behind the dustbins was a pathetic heap of pots and pans, sticks of furniture, bedclothes, broken ornaments and hundreds of folded newspaper spills. This was all there was to show that old Ted and Lizzie had ever lived in that tiny hovel known as number 6, back of 22 Nelson Street. But that was not quite the end of the affair, for I was to see old Lizzie once more.

A new family moved into 6, back of 22. They had lived for years on a coal barge on the Worcester & Birmingham Canal and were glad to get any house, even that one. I assumed that old Ted would have a stone with his name on in the cemetery like our Kevin, but I was never able to find it. Poor old Lizzie could not afford to buy one, I told myself, and dismissed the problem from my mind. Then, one afternoon as I came home from school for my dinner, I caught sight of a familiar figure standing at the bottom of our entry. I would have known that long black coat and battered old hat anywhere. As I got near, old Lizzie spoke to me as though she had never been away.

"'Ello Carole, 'as yer Mom got anythin' ter goo terday?" I stared at her, she looked even older than I remembered. Her long black coat was flapping open and I noticed that under- neath she was wearing a white smock like garment. Printed across it in smudgy black ink were the words 'Winson Green Prison'. I was suddenly scared. What could this mean? Had she committed some crime and been sent to prison? Had she escaped? Archie Hunt's words came back to me, 'She's gorra knife'. I ran past her and down the entry, not stopping until I was in our kitchen.

"Mom. Mom. I've just sin old Lizzie down the entry." I gasped.
"Don't be so bloody daft, she's..."
"But I 'ave Mom. Down the entry. God's honour." I went to church at least twice every Sunday so Mom knew that I would never call down the Lord's name in vain.
"You wait 'ere, I'll goo an' see." I was glad to obey. Mom was back in moments.
"She's locked 'erself in the lavvy but she can't stay in there."

Lizzie had apparently tried to get back into her old home, but the new tenants, naturally, would not let in this strange old woman.

When we went back to school after dinner, us kids used our front door so we would not have to pass the place where Lizzie was hiding. Would I ever dare use those lavatories again, I wondered? But when I came home later Mom put my mind at rest.

"It's all right, they took 'er back, she wunt come round 'ere again." I did not feel like asking who had taken her or where to, but Mom was right, old Lizzie never did come round again.

With the passing of old Ted and the disappearance of Lizzie, it became one of my jobs to take the Monday morning bundles to the pawnshop. It was a job I soon grew to hate because there was always a long queue of women and kids with their parcels. The shop was on the corner of Icknield Street and Summer Hill, opposite the Bullpits [Swan Kettles etc] factory.

The big, plate glass front window was full of gold and silver jewellery, clocks, watches and china ornaments. But this door was only for genuine customers, the bundle bearers had to queue along the side of the building and enter through a dingy back door which led into a small office.

At one end of the office was a metal grill and serving hatch, behind which was an Aladdin's Cave of treasures. Everything under the sun was there from banjos to bicycles, anything that would realise cash. I was not tall enough to reach the hatch, so I had to stand on tiptoe and push my bundle up onto the counter. The name over the shop door was 'Emmanuel Goldfarb', and the man himself was usually on duty at the hatch. He was small, dark and fat with wire trimmed spectacles and a jeweller's eye glass on a cord around his neck. He would open the bundles and examine the contents carefully with maddening thoroughness. Were there any buttons missing, tears or mends, any holes in the shoes or any little thing that might lessen their value? At last he would peer over his spectacles and offer,

"Seventeen and sixpence, take it or leave it." [87.5p] I always took it.

I lost count of the number of times Dad's suit, shirts and shoes went on their holidays over the years, but it was almost every week. Mom used to say,

"If ya never went an' fetched that suit, it'd come back on its own." To the 9 year old me, this conjured up an hilarious picture of Dad's best suit jumping off its coat hanger and running down Icknield Street, hotly pursued by Mr Goldfarb.

Back Trouble

I opened my eyes and saw it not ten feet in front of me, that sad, white face peering in through our bedroom window. It looked like a circus clown, but sadder, and it never took its big watery eyes from me. Joyce and Linda were asleep and of no help at all when the face suddenly moved through the glass and came nearer. I screamed and the effort woke me up. It was a dream I often had, that sad face at the window, staring in at me. Then I heard anoth er strangled scream and Joyce and Linda were instantly awake, looking at me with big eyes, just like the white face.

"Arghhh. Quick Carole... 'elp me." It was Mom's voice.

We were all frightened, but it was me who had to run and see what was happening. I knew that Dad had already gone off to the factory, and so it could not be a row or anything like that. I threw open the door and saw Mom sitting on the edge of the bed, dressed only in her undershirt from the night before. She was quite still with the palm of her hand pressed into the small of her back. With difficulty she turned her head to look at me.

"Carole, me fuckin' back's gone", she gasped. "You'll 'ave ter get the doctor, I can't fuckin' move."

My heart sank at those words, for a visit from the doctor meant that the house would have to be cleaned from top to bottom, by me I turned and yelled out to Joyce and Linda,

"You two gerroff ter school.... Mom's bad." They needed no more encouragement and were soon clumping down the stairs and out of the kitchen door, not wanting to get caught up in this regular trauma. Mom was gingerly trying to move.

"'E can't see me like this.. Get me nightie.......in that drawer." She nodded towards the dressing table and I rummaged around among the stockings, suspenders and underskirts, but no night-dress. "Never mind that then.... you'd better empty the bucket first".

She meant the dreaded slop pail which was full to overflowing from last night at the Nelson. Gently I lifted the bucket and slowly moved towards the door.

"No. Wait a minit…it's there…me nightie, under the fuckin' bed…give it 'ere."

Putting the bucket down, I crawled under the bed and among odd stockings, Mom's fluffy slippers and Dad's second best shoes, was the nightie. It was the Baby Doll type with a frill around the bottom which did not quite reach to Mom's knees. I gave it to her and she sat still, clutching it to her.

"Well goo on then, empty the bucket… an' then you'll 'ave ter goo fer the Doctor … an' gerra fuckin' move on will yer."

As I staggered down the narrow stairs holding the bucket out in front of me, I knew that it was going to be another of those fun days, a day that would mean several hundred trips up and down the stairs while Mom lay in state. In between times I would have to get Kevin up, dress him, feed him and all the rest. Mom's voice followed me down the stairs,

"You'll 'ave to get the dinner Carole… forget about fuckin' school today." I already had.

As I turned Kevin's pushchair back into Nelson Street I pushed faster. It was already 11 o'clock and Dad, Tony and the kids would expect their dinner on time. I could not expect any help from Tony; although he was two years older than me, cooking was girls' work. Liza Hunt had been in to ask Mom if she needed any help, but Mom had told her,

"Oh it's all right Liza, our Carole can manage".

Our Carole was heading home with six pounds of potatoes, two pounds of carrots, three cooking onions and a parcel of pork chops balanced on the pushchair. But the fun was only just beginning. The doctor had been and gone after impressively diagnosing 'a bad back' and prescribing an ointment to rub on it.

With Kevin safely out in the yard in his pushchair, I began to get the dinner ready. We had done a bit on hygiene at school, so before peeling the potatoes I remembered to wash from my hands most of the dark brown greasy ointment I had rubbed on Mom's back. Of course, I had to check everything with Mom first. It went something like this:

"Is this enough water in the potatoes Mom?" I asked holding
the pan for her inspection. She leaned forward painfully.
"Yeah.... now put 'em on a high gas.... 'til they're boiled".
Two minutes later I was back with the pan of carrots.
"D'ya think these are done yet Mom?"
"Done? They're too fuckin' done by the look of 'em. They've
gone all fuckin' soft.... 'ow long 'ave you 'ad 'em on then?"
Then five minutes later holding out the meat tin of chops,
"Cooked? they'll be fuckin' burnt offerin's if yer cook 'em
any more." Then five minutes later, panicking with the gravy
jug and a spoon.
"Mom, I can't get the lumps out of this gravy."
"'Course yer can't. You didn't stir it quick enough when it
come to the boil, you prat."

And so it went on until at last the dinner was cooked, served
and eaten; soft carrots, burnt chops and lumpy gravy. Mom
had hers on a tray in the state room and by the time the meal
was over, her room really was in a state. On the bedside table
were cups and saucers, a full ashtray and the jar of stinking
brown ointment. On the bed was her empty plate, newspaper,
and a cold water bottle waiting for me to refill it. On the floor
was the slop bucket waiting for me to empty it again. The
room which I had made immaculate for the doctor's visit had
reverted to its usual chaos.

The day was wearing on and I was glad, for I knew that Mom
would recover in time for the evening trip to the Nelson. She
always did, and would never let Dad go on his own. Six o'
clock approached and Mom called me upstairs yet again.

"I'm feelin' a bit better now Carole... I'll be gettin' up in a
minit to get yer Dad's tea." I went downstairs, relieved that I
would not have to cook another meal, but Mom's voice
followed, "You'll 'ave ter 'elp me mind."

But the miracle cure was well underway, and by the time Dad
got home Mom was pottering in the kitchen, only occasionally
putting her hand to her back. The only interruption to Dad's
tea this time was Mom telling him in what agony she had been
all day, and how she could not trust me to do anything right.

While they were away at the Nelson I cleaned up the sick room,
putting the jar of ointment into Mom's drawer. That could save
me another trip to the chemist. Looking back, I am almost sure
that these attacks of the bad back were genuine and not just an
excuse to be waited on all day.

The Gas Man Cometh

In our street, the visit of the gas man always caused a stir of
excitement. Mom, Liza and the other women looked forward
to it because it meant a chance of extra cash in the middle
of the week. As soon as he was sighted on his 'sit up and
beg' bicycle, word would spread up and down the street.

"Gas man's comin' Nance, sin 'im outside number siven."
"Carole, tell ya Mom not to goo out, gas man's on 'is way."

The man himself was an impressive sight in his official regalia.
He wore a black cap with shiny peak and silver badge, a black
jacket with silver buttons and his serge trousers were nipped in
tightly at the ankles by his bicycle clips. Over them all he wore
a massive and flapping navy blue raincoat. If we were in the
yard us kids would hear his bike clicking along the entry and
give a loud cheer when he appeared. Down into the cellar he
would go with his massive bunch of jangling keys and come
up with the little metal coin box from the meter. Mom would
clear a space on the kitchen table and he would empty out all
the pennies with a crash. Then he would sit down and count
them into piles of twelve [into shillings], lined up in neat rows.
When he came to the metal washer, Mon would tell him

"Oh, the babby must 'ave put that in, the little bugger." And
when he held up the Irish penny accusingly, "Well, it's so
bloody dark down there I can't see what I'm puttin' in."

The gas man would carefully note the amount collected in a
fat little book held together with elastic bands. Then the dirty
brown pennies would be put into blue paper bags and into his
leather satchel. There would still be a healthy pile of coins
on the table and this was Mom's rebate. The reason for all the
excitement. As soon as he had gone she would sit down and
count her haul. Then Liza would come in.

"'Ow much you got Nance? I got three an' eight." [3s 8d/18.3p]
"There's four an' nine 'ere Liza, that's all right ennit?" [4s 9d/
23.75p]

The gas man's visit could mean the difference between surviving
the week or having food on the strap. Sometimes it could mean a
crafty 'shandy' in the Nelson at dinner time or even an afternoon

trip to the Lyric. The gas man was the one bill collector that everybody welcomed with open arms.

The gas meter in our cellar once caused an even bigger stir than the gas man. If we had a lot of rain, Nelson Street and nearby streets were prone to flooding. There would be several inches of stinking black water in the ground floor rooms of the houses and the meter in our cellar would be under several feet. All furniture that was movable had to be carried up the stairs until the water subsided. When it did, there would be a thick, sticky sludge all through the houses, ruining any carpets and lino. Once it was so bad that Dad's little car floated away and landed up near his factory in Edward Street. Even Dad could see the funny side and I remember him calling upstairs to Mom,

"Hey Nance, I wunt 'ave ter tek the car ter werk this mornin', it's got there before me."

After a day or two of living upstairs and Mom doing the cooking wearing wellington boots, we noticed a very strong smell of gas everywhere, especially from the cellar. There was obviously a leak somewhere, but this was before the days of emergency telephone numbers and instant responses. The gas main was down under the water, but somebody would have to turn it off 'or we'll all bloody goo up with it', as Mom had put it.

Archie Hunt from next door volunteered to go down because he was a strong swimmer. He lost no time in stripping off his shirt and trousers and in just his underpants, plunged into the icy black water. After a few moments he came up looking like a coal miner and shivering violently, but he had managed to turn the gas off. Everybody said how brave he was and Dad gave him ten bob. [10s - 50p] Somehow a local newspaper got wind of it and two reporters turned up and took Archie's photo outside our house. It made the evening edition of the *Despatch* with the headline *'Local Hero Saves Houses in Gas Scare'*.

Poor Archie, it was probably the best thing that ever happened to him. He was always in trouble, and despite the number of beltings he got from Les and Liza, he still went, as they used to say, 'bad ways'. The rod certainly was not spared in Archie's case but they managed to spoil the child. From breaking windows as a kid he graduated to breaking into gas meters, to shoplifting and burglary. He served several terms in Winson Green Prison but nothing seemed to deter him. Years later I came across him in a City centre pub. I barely recognised Archie, but by then I could recognise the face of a heroin addict.

Sitting on the Ice
in the Ice Rink

"Where is it yer goo every Sat'dy mornin' then? Yer never in when I call fer ya.", an exasperated Veronica complained to me one day.
"Ah wouldn't yer like ter know?" I said coyly. I was reluctant to tell her because I knew her next words would be, 'Can I come with yer then?'

Not that I would have minded all that much, but in anything we did Veronica always had to go one better. The truth was that I had seen a Sonia Heine film at the Lyric and watched in amazement and wonder as she skated around doing jumps and turns and spinning so fast that you could hardly see her. I decided there and then that ice skating was for me. As luck would have it, the nearest ice rink was only minutes from home, on the corner of Goodman Street and Spring Hill. From then on, every Saturday morning when I had the money was devoted to teaching myself to skate. I loved that massive rink with the ice cold air wafting up and the coloured lights reflected in it. The latest popular tunes blared from speakers high in the roof as hordes of kids sailed around and around. But it cost sixpence [2.5p] to go in and sixpence to hire the ice skates, so it was only when I had saved a couple of my cleaning sixpences that I could afford it. But I had reached the stage where I could make a complete circuit of the rink without falling down even once. It was time to make Veronica jealous.

"The ice rink?" Veronica's big eyes widened, "You can't skate."
The moment of sweetness had come.
"Oh yes I can, bin gooin' fer wicks, every Sat'dy." She pondered this for a moment then,
"Can I come with yer next wick?"
"Oh, all right" I conceded, but I was determined that she would not have it too easy.

On Saturday morning a nervous Veronica stood tottering on her skates at the edge of the rink watching me flash past. Well, I imagined I was flashing.

"Carole, will ya come round with me so as I can 'old on to yer?"
"All right then, but ya berra learn quick 'cause I ain't draggin' yer round with me all the bloody time.", I told her severely.

85

But when we got out on the ice Veronica was petrified and clung to me like a leech. Every time I shoved her off she sat down on the ice with a bump. 'She'll soon get fed up with this', I thought. Then I pulled her out into the middle of the rink and threatened to skate off and leave her. She panicked.

"Oh no Carole, please don't do that, will ya? I'll 'ave ter slide all the way back on me bum if yer do." The idea of Veronica sliding across the ice on her bum while hordes of kids tried to skate over and around her almost tempted me, but then I remembered I was supposed to be her best friend. Anyway, I told myself, one visit will be enough for her.

But Veronica was not daft and she solved the problem her own way. She got her Mom to pay for skating lessons. The half hour lessons were two shillings [10p] and only kids from the better off families could afford them. But, as I said, Veronica always had to go one better, and she also got her Mom to buy a proper skating outfit. It was a lovely shade of pale green with bands of white fur around the collar and cuffs and matching knickers under a short skirt. She even got brand new ice boots with shining silver skates.

I was the colour of her outfit with envy. She really put my rolled-up-at-the-waist school skirt and navy blue knickers to shame. But even on those Saturdays when I had no money, I still went along to the rink and peered in through a crack in the emergency door at the back. I could just see that part of the ice where Veronica had her lesson, and as I watched her wobbling around in that lovely outfit and brand new ice boots, I promised myself that one day, I would have my very own ice boots.

But it was not until our Tony got his Saturday job at Clements' junk shop that my big chance came. I spotted them in a cardboard box outside the shop. It was a box of things that nobody else seemed to want, but they were definitely ice boots and with skates attached. I asked Tony if he would put them on one side until I had saved up the price of half a crown [12.5p].

"They're no good to yer" he told me. "Them's boys boots, they're black." But I didn't care, they were ice boots weren't they? It took me five weeks of saving my cleaning sixpences without trips to the rink to get those boots.

When I finally took them home and had a close look they did seem just a bit tatty. The boots were cracked and peeling and the skate blades starting to rust, but I set about renovating them with a will. I rubbed off most of the rust with sandpaper and used Tony's football boot dubbin on the cracked leather. Then I rubbed Tony's bike oil all over the blades and they started to look good. But they were still black, and black boots were boys boots, as Veronica would be quick to point out. In the brew house a search among Dad's old paint tins revealed one marked 'white undercoat' which had not gone too hard, and there was a brush that I bashed into softness with the coal hammer. The paint went onto the boots like a dream, covering the black completely after only three or four coats. I thought they looked really great as they dried in front of the kitchen fire. Wouldn't Veronica have a surprise when she saw them?

"Where did yer get them things?" Veronica asked as I proudly skated out onto the ice the very next Saturday morning.
"Wouldn't yer like ter know?"
"They're a bit big ain't they?"

Two sizes too big actually, but I was wearing a pair of Tony's old football socks so they did not slip about too much. I had better not try any jumps though, or I might leave my boots behind. Everything went well until they began to pick up lumps of ice which clung to them. As the ice melted it washed off bits of the white paint until, by the end of the session my boots looked like Dalmatian dogs.

"Them's boys boots.", Veronica laughed triumphantly. Boots or no boots, I consoled myself, I could still skate better than her.

Recently I visited the building just before it was pulled down. After the rink closed it had been a car showroom, a warehouse and more recently by the looks of it, a tramps dormitory. It was in a terrible, dilapidated condition, but I could still trace my route from the pay box up the stairs to the changing rooms, then down to the vast dark area where the ice had been. Now there was only a concrete floor with huge holes that once held the water tanks.

As I stood on the very spot where Veronica and I had skated, laughed and fooled all those years ago, there came a loud crash and a flash of bright light. Was there somebody else in that run down building? Then I saw that the old emergency door at the back of the rink was hanging loose, blowing open and shut in the wind and letting in the occasional shaft of sunlight. It was the same door I had peered through at Veronica having her skating lessons. I had spent many happy hours inside that building and now it is a car park. Pity.

Teacher's Rest and Mother's Pest

Around the end of June each year, Mom would start to get anxious.

"When is it you lot break up then?" she would ask for the tenth time.
"In three weeks.", I would tell her, and Joyce and Linda would give a great cheer.
"An' 'ow lung 'ave yer got?", would be Mom's next question.
"Seven lovely weeks.", another cheer from the kids. Mom looked aghast at this information, as if she had never heard of the long summer holiday.

"Oh God blimey - seven bloody wicks. 'Teacher's rest an' mother's pest.' Well, you'll all 'ave ter find summat ter do, I ain't 'avin' ya under me feet every day." This was usually her next theme and it meant that, besides my chores, I would have to keep our Kevin, Joyce and Linda occupied and out of trouble. It was a vain hope because we seemed to pack more trouble into those seven weeks than the rest of the year put together.

We all say it, at least people of my age and older do; when we were kids the summers were all longer, hotter and happier. Ice cream was creamier, bread tasted like bread, the pop was fizzier and bacon crisper. These are well worn cliches but, I am sure the summers I remember were longer and hotter, or perhaps I have just forgotten the rainy ones.

It would start peacefully enough with us kids, revelling in our new freedom, playing favourite games in the yard from break-fast to bed time. Little Kevin would try to play football with some of the older lads, but they would keep pushing him over and he would start sulking. Joyce and Linda would play hop-scotch with numbers chalked on the yard slabs but the foot-ballers would keep running over them and rubbing them off, and arguments would start. Even if we were all getting on, playing, screaming and laughing together, Mom's experience would cause her to mutter darkly, 'Laughin' in the mornin' means tears before bed', and she was usually right.

My own favourite game was Two Ball, and it depended on having
two unpunctured tennis balls. These were thrown against the yard
wall and caught again with ever increasing speed. If you dropped
one you were 'out' and another girl took over until she dropped
one. There were many variations on the game, but the one I liked
best was Film Stars. You chose the name of a star and for each
letter in the name, a ball had to be thrown and caught again. It
went, 'Shirley Temple was a star ..S...H...I...R...L...E...Y'.
and so on until you had completed the name. It was best to
choose short names, like Tim Holt where seven throws and
catches were involved, rather than say, Esther Williams, with
fourteen. I became very good at Two Ball and graduated to
Three Ball. Very difficult this, and I was one of the few girls
in our area who could do it. My Three Ball days are long past,
but I can still do Two Ball, much to the annoyance of my young
grandson, who can't.

There were hundreds of traditional street games that us kids
could play during those long summer holidays. Games like
O'Grady Says, What's the time Mister Wolf? and Ring Around
the Roses that our parents and grandparents had played in those
same streets and yards. There was a boys only game called Hot
Rice and Cold Semolina that I always wanted to play. The boy
who was 'it' was armed with a tennis ball and had to throw it and
hit one of the other boys, who then became 'it' The game looked
a lot of fun, particularly when the boys would jump up and down
in front of the factory windows on the opposite side of Nelson
Street and taunt the 'it' boy to throw. Usually he gave in to
the temptation, the crash of broken glass would be followed by
an irate voice from the factory, and the street would be deserted
for a few minutes. Then the boys would start the game again on
the other side of the street. But the game lost its attraction when
when irate householders started handing out clips round the ear
to any of the players who came close enough.

The most interesting games were often the ones us kids invented
for ourselves. I had a game that I played by myself in our front
room with the aid of Mom's fire irons, or companion set as it
was called. There was Mister Brush and Mrs Shovel and their
little boy, Tommy Coal Tongs. They all lived happily together
in a little house under the table until Mister Brush got too interested in the highly polished Miss Poker and they all ended up
bashing each other. Now where did I get that idea, I wonder?
Another game I invented was cockroach racing. Joyce, Linda
and me would pick out likely booking bugs at the bottom of our
bedroom wall and see whose choice made it to the ceiling first.

But when Dad installed gas fires in the bedroom, the cockroach population dwindled and these race meetings had to be called off.

Our Tony also had a flair for inventing games. These were usually designed to show him in a good light and make every-body else look silly. Either that, or the object would be to inflict grievous bodily harm on me, my sisters or any of the other kids who would stand for it. When the complaints came, Tony could claim,

"Aw Mom, it's only a game."

One of Tony's games was Jumping the Broomstick. He would take hold of Mom's big, wooden yard broom by the very end of its long handle. Standing in one spot, he would twirl the brush end in a circle, skimming over the paving slabs at about knee height. Faster and faster he would twirl, and kids playing had to jump over the broom. If they were hit they were 'out', sometimes in more ways than one. From Tony's point of view this was the perfect game, but after falling for it a few times the rest of us got tired of the pain of bruised knees and skinned ankles and refused to play. Tony would point at us, shout,

"Chicken the lorrof ya.", flapping his arms and make clucking noises.
"Well, let us do the broom for a change then.", we would say, but Tony was having none of that.
"Naw, you lot can't turn it fast enough."

One morning as Mom was getting the dinners, we let Tony talk us into having another go at his favourite game. The fact that he promised a threepenny bit [1.25p] to the one who was last to be out had something to do with it. When Tony started to twirl Betty, Joyce, Linda and me started in the circle, but Linda, the youngest and smallest, was soon out. She screamed with pain as the broom thumped into her ankle and the noise attracted Mom's attention.

"An' you can shut that fuckin' row up." From the clashing of pots and pans it sounded as though dinner was not going well.

Linda retreated to the brew house to nurse her injury and moan out of Mom's earshot. The broom twirling and jumping began again and the next to be hit was Betty, right on her knee. With a shrill scream she limped to the doorstep and sat down clutching her leg.

"Bloody 'ell Tony, yer doin' it too bloody fast.", she complained.
"Tony whatever it is yer doin', fuckin' pack it in.", came Mom's
voice from the depths of the kitchen.
"Aw, it's only a bloody game Mom." shouted Tony, grinning to
himself.

Now there was only Joyce and me left 'in', both with our minds
firmly fixed on the promised threepenny bit. But Joyce was not
quick enough and the broom caught her a heavy knock on the
ankle. Wailing loudly she hobbled into the kitchen.

"Hey Mom, tell our Tony, he's killin' us with that broom."
"Tony bring that fuckin' broom in 'ere.... now." Mom ordered. I
was the only broom jumper left and by rights, the threepence was
mine. But Tony was crafty. With a quick glance towards the
kitchen door, he said "C'mon, one more goo and then you're the
winner".

I don't know why I agreed, but I did. I wanted that threepence
and Tony was equally determined that I should not have it. Faster
and faster he twirled the broom, but each time I managed to jump
over it. Tony was red faced and sweating and I could see that he
was slowing down, I was going to be the winner. But Tony still
had a trick up his sleeve. As the broom got near me the next
time, he raised it a couple of feet and caught me hard and high
on the thigh. He yelled in triumph,

"You're out." I stood there holding my leg and though
"Right, I'll fuckin' fix you, ya twistin' sod." But when I ran
into the kitchen. I had no idea just how well he would be fixed.

"Hey Mom, tek that broom off our Tony, will ya? He's bloody
mad. Look 'ere..." I pulled up my skirt to show the red patch on
my thigh where the broom had hit. Joyce pulled down her sock
and showed a skinned ankle. Mom slammed down the saucepan,

"Right, that's fuckin' it."

It is a well worn phrase, but Tony really did not know what hit
him. One minute he was cockily balancing the broom on the palm
of his hand, and the next Mom had snatched it off him and brought
the business end down on his head with a terrible, hollow 'clonk'.
Joyce and me watched from the kitchen and our grins fell away
as we saw the blood spurt from Tony's scalp, pour down his face
and spatter his shirt front. Mom did not turn around until she
was half way back to the kitchen.

"Oh my God, I didn't mean to 'it 'im that 'ard." She led the
dazed Tony inside and tried to staunch the blood with a tea
towel.
"On Christ, he'll 'ave ter goo up the 'ospital now." Mom was
already on a second tea towel but the bleeding would not stop.
"Carole, you goo up an' get her Dad out the factory quick."

As I ran down Edward Street, two men were unloading sheets of
metal from a lorry. When they saw me coming they called out to
Dad who was inside. He came out wiping his hands on a dirty rag
and asked in his usual resigned way,

"Well, what's 'appened now then, gell?" I told him about Tony's
head but left out the part about Mom and the broom. She would
have to explain that herself.

Back in the kitchen Tony was still holding the tea towel to his
head while Mom wiped his face over with the flannel to 'mek him
a bit respectable' for his trip to Dudley Road Hospital.

"Now don't worry son, you'll be all right, goo with yer Dad and
keep pressin' the towel to it..." Mom watched them head for the
front door with anxious eyes, then she remembered something.
"An' don't you dare tell 'em 'ow it 'appened or I'll fuckin' kill
ya."

Mon and Kevin in the kitchen at Alexandra Road.

Love, Death and Rock 'n' Roll

Hidden in the corner of our yard, between the brew house door
and the mangle, Joyce, Betty and me stood passing around a
little pink plastic telescope. Each time it was our turn to peer
into it we shrieked with laughter. Linda, who was the youngest,
ran around trying to snatch it away and see what the excitement
was about. The telescope contained about a dozen little coloured
pictures which changed when you pressed a button on the side.

"Look at 'er then, she ain't got nuthin' on."
"'Ave you sin the size of 'ers, they must be falsies."
"Huh, don't think much of 'ers, mine are bigger than that."
"Gerraway Linda, you're too bleedin' young."
"I'm gonna tell Mom if you don't let me look then..."
"Oh goo on then, but only press it once."

The pictures in the little telescope were innocent enough by
today's standards, girls with their bikini tops off and some not
even facing the camera. But in those days before 'page three'
girls, top shelf magazines and videos, it was pretty hot stuff.
Quite soon our laughter and shrieks drew Mom's attention.

"What yer got there, then?" She stood at the kitchen door, arms
folded across her floral pinnie.
"Nothin' Mom," I said, stupidly putting the telescope behind my
back.
"C'mon, gee it 'ere." Mom held out her hand and there was no
escape. She took it from me, stared at it for a moment then
pressed it to her eye, squinting. "Can't see nothin'..." she
complained.
"You gorra press the button Mom," I told her. She did so and I
saw her face change. She looked down at me for a moment then
rack into the telescope.

"It's bleedin' filth," she said without taking her eye away. She
pressed the button a few more times then turned to me. "Where
the 'ell did you gerrit?"
"Gell at school lent it me Mom, but I gorra tek it back...." Mom
waved the offending toy in front of my face. "It's bleedin'
filth."
"But Mom it's only...", but she was not listening, she had
disappeared back into the kitchen taking the telescope with her.

93

I saw Mom throw the telescope into the flames of the kitchen fire and stared in horror as it bent and twisted in the heat, then flared up with bright orange flames. After a few moments all that was left was a pool of pink melted plastic running down the hot coals.

"Mom, it ain't mine... it's that gell's.... I gorra tek it 'er back." But Mom was fiercely plastering Echo margarine on the bread for Dad's tea, indignation in her every stroke of the knife. "You're gooin' bloody bad ways, you are. Gettin' in the puddin' club afore long, you will."

I had only a vague idea of what she meant and could not understand why she was so angry. After all, they were just some old pictures of girls showing their tits, and I was a girl wasn't I? I was about to make the point when Mom cut me short with a wave of the bread knife.

"It's bleedin' filth." she repeated in a tone that discouraged further queries. I went back outside to the kids and told them what had happened.

"Whooooah. What you gonna tell that gell who lent it ya?" "Dunno... oh yeah, I'll tell 'er that me Mom's gorrit. She wunt ask 'er ferrit back, will she?"

In fact, the girl who had lent me the telescope had pinched it off her brother who had bought it from a dirty book shop in Birmingham. When he brought it to school it caused quite a sensation, for there was literally more to it than met the eye. All round the eyepiece of the telescope was a pad covered with black inky stuff. All the girls had been let in on this secret but not the boys. They were only too eager to get a look at 'the nudes', and it went around the playground like wildfire. That afternoon most of the boys were sporting black eyes, and the girls shrieked with laughter and pointed at them, calling,

"We know what you've bin doin', ya dirty bugger." Their bewildered looks were really something to see.

But now the telescope was gone and I would have to face its owner in the morning. There was another problem. Would it be before or after they set out for the Nelson that Mom would notice her own black eye? And when she did, would she connect it to telescope and me?

"Bloody filth." Mom had branded those harmless pin up pictures, but that was how all the adults I knew reacted to matters sexual. It seems very odd now, especially in an area where sexual swear words were the norm, child abuse not uncommon and illegitimate births frequent. I can't remember any sex education lessons at school and there were certainly none at home. Any queries in that direction would bring a clout around the ear and a threat to 'wash yer mouth out with carbolic soap'.

I was now 11, going on 12, and the only information on sex I had came from overheard dirty jokes, most of which I did not understand, although I pretended I did. I also had what some of the older girls in the street told me, but most of this did not seem to make much sense either. My friends seemed to know as little as I did, perhaps that is why many of them got pregnant even before leaving school. On the pictures it was simple. The hero always fell in love with the prettiest girl, they kissed and it faded out. Simple. So watching film actors and actresses kiss was the limit of my sexual knowledge; beyond that was the great unknown.

It was about this time that Mom started to give me stern but mysterious warnings about what happened to girls who let boys 'mess about' or 'interfere' with them. What this might involve was never explained. I was curious but confused, and I somehow got the idea into my head that kissing could make you pregnant. Lots of girls I knew believed this and it naturally put me right off any form of physical contact with boys. I even considered touching a bit too risky. Anyway, I was not interested in boys, I told myself, although they certainly seemed to be finding me interesting. They would creep up behind me in the playground to lift my dress and laugh at my knickers, which often had the broken elastic tied in a bow at the front. During playground scuffles they never seemed to miss the opportunity of giving me soft punches on my swelling breasts and they loved pulling my long plaits.

But I could not think why boys should get interested in me. After all, I looked in the mirror often enough to know that I was revoltingly ugly. Why were my eyes all squashed up and squinty? Why did my cheekbones stick out so much. And why, when I smiled, did I look like our piano with the lid open? I had always tried to model myself on Flash Gordon's girl friend, the blonde and beautiful Dale Arden, but thought I looked more like the Emperor Ming. I was worried enough to ask Mom.

"Mom, why don't I look like all the other kids? Why do I look...
Chinese?" Mom gaped at me then laughed.
"Chinese? Don't be so bloody daft. An' ya better not let ya Dad
'ear ya say that." she warned. But I was not convinced. I still
have my school photo for that year and I definitely look Chinese.
I am not sure, but perhaps I still do.

It was at this time that I first met Dennis. One night after school
I was skipping in our yard with Betty when a strange boy came
down the entry. About 12 with dark curly hair and blue eyes, he
wore a smart green cord jacket with shiny buttons, matching short
trousers, long socks with no wrinkles or 'taters' in them, and
highly polished brown boots. Betty and me looked at each other.
Who could this handsome stranger be? Then he spoke and we both
knew that this was what we had seen on the pictures - love at
first sight.

"Excuse me gorls, I wonder if you could help me now. I'm lookin'
for the Hunts, so I am." He spoke in a soft Irish accent and was
so polite it seemed unreal. Betty was the first to recover.

"Yeah, that's me... I mean us. Me Mom's inside, c'mon I'll tek
ya." They disappeared into the kitchen and I was left fretting
and fuming in the yard. Next day at school I lost no time in
questioning Betty.

"Well, 'is name's Dennis, 'e's me Mom's sister's lad an' guess
what?" I couldn't so she told me. "They've come ter live in Summer 'ill, an' he's comin' to our school."

It was almost too good to be true. But wait a minute, I thought,
Dennis could not marry me *and* Betty could he? I thought about
this problem all day until something Betty had said gave me an
idea. In a roundabout way I broached the subject with Mom and
she innocently gave me the answer I was looking for. After school
I called for Betty but avoided the subject of Dennis until I
thought she was off her guard.

"Y'know that Dennis bloke?"
"Yeah, worrabout 'im?"
"Well, 'e's yer cousin ain't 'e?"
"Course 'e 'is, so what?" I went in for the kill.
"Well, you can't marry yer cousin, didn't ya know?"
"Oh yeah. 'Oo ses so?"
"Me Mom ses it's against the law ter marry ya cousin, that's 'oo."
"An' 'ow would she know?" I was ready for this.

"'Cause 'er cousin wanted ter marry 'er, an' they wouldn't let 'im, that's how." Betty thought about this for a moment, then said,
"Don't wanna fuckin' marry 'im anyroad." She walked sulkily away.

So that was all right then. So far, so good. But then Veronica had a go. I saw her on Dennis's first day at our school, standing looking up at him with those big brown eyes and he was obviously interested. This was a time for direct action. I ran over and grabbed Dennis from behind by the snake belt that held up his cord trousers. I pulled him into the privacy of the bike shed. He was certainly surprised, but not annoyed.

"What you talkin' to 'er for?" I asked.
"Veronica? Oh she just asked me where I come from, so she did."
"Now she'll tell everybody you're 'er boyfriend... she always does."

Dennis looked surprised but made no attempt to go back to Veronica. It had worked, I was learning to be a woman at last. And that is how Dennis became my first boyfriend and I became his girlfriend. But certainly no kissing, I knew very well where that could lead.

Dennis was different from the other boys. He was clean and tidy, friendly and polite. He was never rude or 'talked dirty' and even Mom took a liking to him.

"At least 'e's got some fuckin' manners." Praise indeed from Mom.

Dennis and his mom had come from London to the little terraced house in Summer Hill so that she could be near her sister Liza Hunt. Dennis's father was in the Navy and rarely home, and his mom obviously doted on him, an only child, which was a rarity in Ladywood.

Some school dinner times, Dennis would take me back to his house and his mom would make us banana sandwiches that we ate sitting on his front doorstep watching the traffic. Dennis was always full of surprises. One dinnertime as we set off for his house, he turned to me and said,

"I've got a monkey now y'know Carole". I stared at him but he was not grinning.
"A monkey? Y'mean like in the zoo?" I asked in amazement.

97

"Yeah, me Mom got it for me birthday, so she did." I still didn't believe him until we got to his back door. His mother was outside peering in through the tiny kitchen window and she was obviously upset.

"Oh Dennis I'm so glad you're home.. he's gone mad.. jumping all over the place... I can't get a hold of him and he's doin'.... 'it' everywhere, so he is."

We peered in through the window but at first it was too dark to see anything. Then a sudden movement caught my eye and a real live monkey swung down from the light fitting and landed by the sink. Now I could see that it was dressed in a little blue romper suit. There was a small metal badge pinned to the front and I could just make out the words 'Arsenal Football Club'. A football supporting monkey in a blue suit going mad in a kitchen in Summer Hill.... no one would ever believe me.

I tapped on the glass and the monkey stopped its antics and stared at me. He looked quite bewildered, poor thing. Then I noticed a pan of potatoes at the side of the sink and suddenly remembered. I had errands to fetch for Mom that dinnertime. I would have loved to have stayed and get better acquainted with the little blue monkey, but duty called and I left Dennis and his mom to face it alone and ran all the way back to Nelson Street. I did try to tell Mom and the kids about what I had seen but I was right, they did not believe me, even leaving out the part about the romper suit and badge.

Not long after the business of the mad monkey, there was an incident at school which showed that Dennis was really quite fond of me. He must have been to risk so much. One of the few male teachers at Nelson Street School was a Mr Goss and all the kids were scared of him. He was a small, dark man with a little moustache and he never missed an opportunity to slap, cane or slipper any child who misbehaved, no matter how minor their offence. The kids all called him Hitler and he made matters worse by sometimes behaving very oddly during lessons. One day in an English lesson there was no more noise in the classroom than usual, but suddenly Mr Goss whirled around from the blackboard and barked,

"Right, I'll cane the next child to speak." We all kept quiet because we knew that he would carry out his threat at the slightest excuse. Mr Goss then sat down at his desk and covered his face with his hands. Someone had told us that he had had a bad time during the war and had never recovered properly, but this did not mean much to us.

Dennis was sitting right behind me, and he leaned forward and gently pulled one of my plaits in an effort to get my attention quietly. I had been miles away, staring at the despairing figure of Mr Goss, wondering what was the matter. At Dennis's touch I started violently and screamed out loud. Mr Goss's head shot up,

"Carole Biddle, come out here." As I walked slowly to the front of the class, I saw Mr Goss take a man's white gym pump from his desk drawer and flex it in his hands. He indicated an empty desk in the front row. "I warned you, didn't I? Now bend over."

With burning cheeks I leaned over the desk top trying not to catch the eye of any of the kids, especially Dennis's. I stared hard at the scratch marks and ink stains on the desk lid as I waited for the pain to come. But it didn't, and I heard the scraping of a chair and suddenly Dennis's voice sounded very close to me.

"You mustn't hit Carole with that Mr Goss, it was my fault, so it was." He spoke softly but firmly and I looked up to see Mr Goss's pale face staring at him in amazement.

"Get back to your seat lad." he croaked, but Dennis did not move. Mr Goss made a sudden movement with the slipper, but Dennis was too quick for him. Snatching it out of Mr Goss's hand, he flung it towards the blackboard where it hit with a loud thwack. For a long moment the three of us stood transfixed, and I remember the rows of startled kids' faces.

Dennis was the first to recover. He grabbed me by the wrist and pulled me from the classroom. We ran down the deserted corridor and out into the playground, and did not stop running until we were across Nelson Street and in the safety of Mom's kitchen.

"What the bloody 'ell's 'appened now then?" she wanted to know. Mom looked from one to the other as we tried to explain about Mr Goss, my plait, the slipper and how Dennis had saved me. When we finished our story, to my surprise Mom said,

"That bloody bugger." It was a relief to have her on our side. "You tek no notice. If anybody comes over 'ere, I'll see 'em." she told us.

That was all right then, but I was still scared when we went into school the next morning. But the day wore on and there was no summons for me or Dennis to the headmaster's office, and Mr Goss did not come looking for us. We had got away with it.

Shortly after this it went round the school that Mr Goss had been sacked because there had been complaints about his slippering other girls. I do not know if this was true, but we never saw Mr Goss or his slipper again. Dennis became something of a hero for his daring deed. Our Tony had started at the big school some two years previously but he remembered Mr Goss, and when I told him about Dennis and the slipper, he laughed and said,

"Old man Goss? I 'ated that bugger, good 'ole Dennis." After this Tony and Dennis became mates.

Moke fever was sweeping the country and the local lads were soon caught up in it. In fact these were just the old fashioned soap box carts with a new name. Two sets of wheels from an old pram or pushchair were fastened to a plank of wood about four feet long. Onto this was nailed a Ffyfes banana box in which the driver sat. Steering was by a loop of rope fastened to either side of the front axle and the Mokes were driven by push power. Downhill and on the straight they could get up quite a speed. Tony and Dennis quickly became enthusiastic and expert Moke builders. No sooner had they smashed up one but they were scavenging bits for the next, which was always going to be better, bigger and faster.

One Friday night after school I was sitting in our yard watching Tony work on his latest Moke when Dennis came down the entry. Under his arm he was carrying a set of pram wheels which must have come from an expensive model, because they had fat tyres of solid rubber. Tony looked them over enviously and asked Dennis what he intended to do with them.

"I'm startin' a new Moke with these, me old one's smashed up but this one will do a hundred with these when it's finished." He held up the new wheels. Tony laughed at his confidence.
"You bugger off, it wunt beat this 'un." he grinned, twirling the wheels with his hands.
"All right then Tony, when mine's finished, we'll have a race, so we will, then we'll see who's fastest." Dennis winked at me as he made the challenge.
"Yer on. But you got no chance mate." Tony grinned. Dennis turned to me.

"I'll see ya tomorrow Carole, I'll come call for you, I will."
With that, he disappeared down the entry carrying his new Moke
wheels, and I never saw him again.

It was Saturday afternoon and I had nearly given up on Dennis.
Maybe they had more monkey trouble or something. I was wondering if I ought to go round to Summer Hill and see what had
happened when there was a knock at our front door. This was
unusual, for the people we knew always came to the back door.
Mom went to answer it closing the door behind her, and I was
just about to go out into the yard when I heard the sound of a
woman's voice from the front room. I moved closer to the door;
whoever our caller was she sounded upset, distraught even. Her
voice sounded vaguely familiar and I was able to catch just a
few words, but they were enough. Something about 'Dennis…
main road…bus driver had no chance…died instantly'.

The next thing I remember was waking up in the armchair with
Mom trying to push a green glass bottle of smelling salts under
my nose. When she had come back to the kitchen I was stretched
out on the lino; I must have fainted dead away. The next few days
are just a blurred memory. I was kept off school, in bed most of
the time, I cried a lot and slept a lot. Joyce and Linda were kept
out of my way and I had no chores to do. Everything had an air of
unreality and this new experience of grief shook me so much that
I was sorry I had ever met Dennis. I just wanted to get back to
normal, whatever that was. Anything was better than the awful
limbo that I found myself in with nothing to occupy me but
thoughts of Dennis.

Dennis's funeral procession passed along Nelson Street and
halted for a time outside the school so the kids could pay their
last respects. I knew nothing about this until long afterwards
because Mom kept me in bed all that day. It was some time
later that I learnt the details of how Dennis had died.

He had finished his new Moke and with some other Irish lads
from Summer Hill had gone off to try it out. They all had Mokes
and decided to race, in preparation for the proposed race against
our Tony's new Moke. For some unknown reason they had chosen
a steep hill which ran down under a railway arch. But Icknield
Street was a main bus route, and as they raced into the darkness
under the bridge they were invisible to the driver of the oncoming
bus. It hit Dennis first. His mates following on were badly hurt
but eventually recovered. By a strange coincidence, the accident
happened outside Warstone Lane Cemetery where Dennis was
buried.

The accident was reported in all the local papers and there were calls for Mokes to be banned. Mom would not let me see any of the news reports or read about the inquest, but as soon as I was up and about again, I made myself go and look at that stretch of Icknield Street that ran under the railway bridge. I did not want to believe that Dennis would have been so stupid as to race his Moke down the middle of a main road, and I knew that he had not been. They had started on the wide pavement at the top of the hill, but had been in the middle of the road when the bus had hit them. Half way down the hill I found a possible answer. Here the pavement had crumbled away and there was no gutter, just a rough ramp. A Moke at speed would have been diverted out into the road by the ramp, just like a train going over the points. But my detective work gave me little comfort, Dennis was still dead.

As I did after the death of the first Kevin, I began to hang around the cemetery a lot. This was the third time in my young life that the thing called death had touched me on the shoulder, and it was certainly the worst. I had been too young to feel any grief at Kevin's death. They told me that he had gone to heaven and I was glad for him, it was a nice place to be, so they told me. Old Ted had just been a wax doll who did not move anymore, but Dennis had been real. I knew how he had looked, how he walked and talked and laughed and played. Now there was nothing to show for all that, but a stone with his name on it. And just what was it that I had felt for Dennis? Was it real love, like they had on the pictures? I had no way of knowing. If he had lived would we have got married and lived in Lady-wood and had lots of kids and lots of rows, like everyone else?

Touchingly, Dennis's mom had wanted me to have his little blue monkey, Jimmy. But I would not see her and it was Mom who saved me the painful job of telling her that I could not take Jimmy. He was no substitute for Dennis and he would only remind me. Besides, I could just imagine Dad's face if he came home from work to find an Arsenal supporting monkey in front of our kitchen fire with the rest of the menagerie. Not that he had anything against monkeys, but Dad was a Birmingham City supporter. Ah well - I could still smile.

Something else happened in that crowded year of 1956 that helped to take my mind of my troubles, something which would change the lives of thousands of youngsters for ever. A fat, middle aged man in a grey suit with a lock of greasy hair hanging over his forehead sang a song called *Rock Around The Clock*, and suddenly teenagers were born.

It is hard now to imagine a world without teenage music, fashions, magazines, films and TV programmes, but until the mid 1950s and rock'n'roll, boys and girls in their teens were just miniatures of their parents. Girls in Ladywood wore hand me downs from elder sisters or mother, and even new clothes were purchased from the same shops, and in much the same styles, as their mothers and grandmothers. Boys who wanted to look grown up borrowed dad's old gabardine raincoat and trilby hat, both a couple of sizes too big. Popular entertainment was dominated by middle aged men and women. Victor Sylvester, Edmundo Ross and Donald Peers topped the hit parade along with Gracie Fields and Vera Lynn; even my old mate George Formby was still going strong. But Bill Hayley and His Comets changed all that forever.

I was 11 going on 12, so I did not fully appreciate the enormity of what was happening, but for kids just a few years older than me about to go out and earn money for the first time in their lives, it opened up a new world of freedom, independence and opportunity that they had never known before. Even for me, it was certainly an interesting time to be young.

I had mixed feelings about rock'n'roll music. Yes, it was loud and exciting and all the kids seemed to love it, but you could not really sing along to it as I had done with those old gramophone records in our front room. But Tony was nearly three years older than me and really caught the rock'n'roll bug. He got himself a Saturday job in a local junk shop and bought his first record player, a pink and grey Dancette with a tiny speaker in the detachable lid. The seven and sixpence [37.5p] that he earned on Saturdays was usually spent on the latest pop records which he would play at full blast on the Dancette in our yard at night.

Tony even taught me to jive, or bop, as they called it then. Being small and lightweight, he could throw me around all over the place, just like we had seen on TV or the pictures. Often I was just too tired to do much dancing. I still had all my chores to do, Kevin to look after, errands to run and church and school to go to. So Tony got himself a girl friend, the first of many, but I noticed with satisfaction that he did not throw her around as much as he had me; she was bigger and heavier.

For me, puberty was approaching fast to play havoc with my hormones. I did not realise that this new era of teenage freedom and independence would bring even more restrictions and responsibilities for Carole Biddle.

The Big School

As the long summer holiday of 1956 drew to a close, Veronica and me were both looking forward to starting together at 'the big school'. This was to be Follet Osler Girls' Secondary, which was in Clarke Street not far from Nelson Street. The main reason I was looking forward to it was that the school was very close to Monument Road swimming baths and, money permitting, I would be able to go there straight from school two or three times a week.

Swimming was my favourite recreation and I had taught myself to swim when I was about 7, or rather I had taken the Tony Biddle 'Swim in a Day' splash course. This consisted of our Tony and his mates throwing me bodily into the deep end of the pool, and when I struggled out, throwing me in again.

In the mornings Veronica would call for me and we would take a short cut along the canal to come up in Monument Road. Follet Osler was only a short walk away. The building was of red brick and to us seemed very old. It was topped by an ancient bell tower that was a familiar landmark around the district. The headmistress was a dark haired Irish lady called Mrs McLoughlin. She had a false foot following a war time injury, so naturally the girls called her Peg Leg. But Follet Osler was not to be a happy place for me. I had lost so much time at Nelson Street School that most lessons were an embarrassing mystery. At cookery, sewing, domestic science and swimming I was brilliant, but at anything else I was hopeless.

One of the teachers at Follet Osler made an immediate impression on me. Mrs Reeves, the maths teacher, was tall, slim and always immaculately dressed with her long nails carefully manicured. She was unlike any other teacher or adult that I had ever met. Every morning she parked her little bright pink bubble car on the same spot in the playground, and I mean exactly the same spot. Veronica and me would wait for her to arrive and watch to see if she got it right. She always did, to the very inch. She was obviously very fond of her little car and spent most break times polishing the pink paintwork and the transparent dome, or sweeping out the inside with a special little brush.

I was hopeless at mathematics and was glad that Mrs Reeves did not seem all that keen on the subject either. Sometimes she

would come into the classroom and say,
"I've had my hair done girls, what do you think? Too much on
top?", and she would listen to our opinions. Or she would walk
up and down at the front of the class and ask us

"Do you think this outfit suits me girls. A bit too short perhaps?"

Informality from a teacher was something I had never come across
before. Often she would abandon the lesson all together, draw up
her chair to the front row of desks and talk about herself. She
told us all about her husband, how they met, the holidays they
had taken together and how he had been one of the first to join
up when war came. She told us what a wonderful man he was,
but when she came to the part about him being posted by his unit
'missing, believed killed', the tears would stream down her face
while we shuffled our feet in embarrassed silence, hoping that
the bell would ring for the end of the lesson. But we all liked
Mrs Reeves and felt sorry about her husband.

Then one morning there was no pink bubble car parked precisely
in the playground and there would be no more informal chats
with Mrs Reeves. We never saw her again, and for a long time no
other member of staff mentioned her. It was some weeks later that
I was sitting in our kitchen finishing my jam sandwich while Mom
read the *Evening Mail*. Suddenly, she put the paper down and stared
at me.

"'Ave you gorra teacher called Mrs Reeves?"
"Yeah, but she's bin off a bit, why?"

Without a word she passed me the paper, and I was startled to see
Mrs Reeves' face. She looked younger than when I had known her
and was smiling happily. The caption read, 'Inquest on teacher'.
I had no idea what an inquest might be, but as I stumbled through
the piece with a growing dread, I realised that Mrs Reeves was
dead. Then I came to a bit about her husband and my scalp
crawled.

He had not been killed during the war as Mrs Reeves had believed,
but survived, returned to England and married someone else under
an assumed name. For some reason that I could not make out, he
had recently contacted her to confess the truth. The shock had
been too much, she had driven her beloved car deliberately and
at speed into a wall and been killed instantly. The verdict was
'suicide while the balance of the mind was disturbed'.

I was shocked at her death and at the verdict. They were saying that our Mrs Reeves had been 'barmy' when she did what she did, but how could they know what her mind was like after her husband turned up? All her illusions, all her memories, wiped out. I thought that it was all very unfair on Mrs Reeves as she had probably thought what she was doing would be for the best, and who could say that it was not? Once again death had claimed someone I knew, but had never really got to know. At school we were all upset about what had happened to Mrs Reeves but, much as I liked her, I could shed no tears for her, I had shed all mine for Dennis.

Miss Poole, the art mistress, was another teacher that I came to like very much. Thankfully nothing happened to her, and it was Miss Poole who was responsible for the happiest moment in my four years at the school.

One morning assembly the teacher hierarchy were in their usual chairs on the platform. The girls stood in rows whispering and giggling, nudging each other and nodding towards the ample form of Miss Dunsby, the history teacher. Usually at this time of the morning her knickers were on display as she sat carelessly splay legged. Then the headmistress swept in, or as much of a sweep as she could manage with her gamy leg. She stumped up onto the platform smiling broadly.

"Good morning girls." she said nodding to us. This was the signal that we could all sit down on the floor.
"Good morning Miss McLoughlin." we chorused dutifully.
"As you will all have noticed, we have something new to catch our eyes this morning." I had noticed nothing but wondered if Miss Dunsby had bought a new pair of knickers. Before I could give it any further thought she went on, "Will Carole Biddle please stand up."

I was panic stricken as my mind raced over the events of the last few days. Surely I had not done anything that bad? She was not going to expel me in front of the whole school, was she? But worse was to follow.

"Please come up onto the platform Carole." she ordered. With flaming cheeks I made my slow way past the rows of girls with three hundred pairs of eyes boring into my back. Up those four wooden steps I went with a sinking heart, until I stood in front of the headmistress, eyes downcast.

"This is the girl", she boomed, "this is the girl we have to thank for brightening up our hall this morning."

I gaped at her, head swimming. Had she gone mad and mistaken me for one of the cleaners? Then I noticed that the other girls were looking around the hall, at the dozens of pictures of all shapes and sizes that now covered the flaking cream paintwork.

"Every one of these lovely paintings was done by Carole and I think that she deserves a round of applause.", beamed Miss McLoughlin.

I did not know whether to laugh or cry as the headmistress shook me by the hand and, weak with relief, I was allowed to slip back into the anonymous rows of girls. Looking round surreptitiously, I could hardly believe I had painted all these landscapes, sunsets, street scenes, kids playing, Dad's car, animals, birds and all the others. I had forgotten most of them, but dear Miss Poole had carefully saved all my work. That morning, she had come in early to decorate the hall with them and surprise me. It was quite a surprise, it was also the best thing that ever happened to me at school. I could not wait to get home and tell Mom and the kids about my one girl exhibition at the school, only our Tony was unimpressed.

"Huh, they can't be much good if you done 'em."

A few days later there was a parent evening at the school and I asked Mom if she and Dad would come and see my paintings.

"'Ow can we? I gorra get yer Dad's tea and we gorra get our-selves ready." She meant to go down the pub. I was disappointed but not surprised. But the very next day at break time I was more than surprised to see the familiar figure of Mom come in through the school gates.

"Mom, what are you doin' 'ere?" I asked her in some alarm.
"Come ter see yer werk ya told me about. In the 'all ennit?"
"Yeah, but yer can't goo in there on yer own. I'll 'ave ter ask the teacher."
"Gerroff, I ain't got no time ter mess about, I gorra get back fer the dinner" and in she marched with me tagging fearfully behind, praying that nobody would try to stop her.

I think that she was a bit bemused by the sheer number of my paintings on display and the diversity of subjects. And I know that she was wondering what help all this would be when I came to get a job in one of the local factories. But I was very glad that she had bothered to come and look.

Things I Didn't Know
I Didn't Know

Our Tony was always a keen comic collector. All around his bed in the attic were neat piles of *Beanos, Dandys, Film Fun* and *Knockout*. As he got older he added *The Eagle, Adventure, Wizard* and *Hotspur*. Tony guarded his comic collection jealously and would never let the rest of us kids look at or even touch them.

His attic bedroom was strictly out of bounds, but sometimes, when Mom kept me off school, I would creep up there, sit on his bed and leaf through my favourite stories of Biffo the Bear, Lord Snooty or Dan Dare - Pilot of the Future. I would always put them back exactly as I had found them, even smoothing out the bed where I had been sitting, but he always knew.

Tony would come in from school, clump up to his attic, then clump down again a few moments later. Suddenly I would feel a sharp clout round my ear with Tony's voice behind me.

"Leave me bleedin' comics alone will ya.?"
"Piss off. I ain't even bin up there."

"Oh yes you 'ave an' next time I'll fuckin' kill ya." So much for brotherly love. But how did he know? Perhaps he stretched cotton across the attic doorway as I had seen Sherlock Holmes do in a film? I never found out.

When Tony got his Saturday job at a junk shop and bought his first record player, piles of second hand pop records took their place with his comics. He would spend most of his seven and sixpence wages [37.5p] before he even left the shop. One Saturday night Tony came staggering in with his usual carrier bag full of records and other junk that he had bought. I ignored him because I was sick of him going on about what he had bought or was going to buy with his rotten seven and six. But this time, instead of hauling the booty up to his attic lair, he turned to me and asked

"You wanna job then?" I did not answer him at first, thinking it was only one of his stupid jokes and that he had a smart answer ready when I said yes. I was still cautious when he repeated the question.

"What d'ya mean a job?"

"The old gell from the clothes shop come across and asked me if I knew anybody. I said I'd tell ya."

The junk shop where Tony worked was owned by an old man named Clements, and by a strange coincidence it was on the corner of Clemence Street, just two streets along the Parade from where we lived. Across the main road was a little haberdashery shop run by a middle aged Jewish couple called Goodman. It was Mrs Goodman who had spoken to Tony.

"You gorra werk from nine 'til six an' she's payin' ten bob", Tony told me. Ten bob. [ten shillings - 50p] Ten whole shillings, all to myself every week. I could hardly believe it. Me, who earned only an occasional sixpence for cleaning neighbours' houses. Ten bob was beyond riches.

"Ya gorra goo an' see 'er on Monday if you wanna do it.", Tony went on. I came down to earth with a bump.
"Huh, she wunt let me, will she?" I said jerking my head in the direction of the kitchen where Mom was pottering about.
"I dunno, goo an' ask 'er.", replied Tony, and promptly lost interest.

I wandered into the kitchen where Mom was cutting doorstep slices of bread for Dad's evening meal. The interview did not start too well.

"Mom, ya know Goodman's clothes shop along the Parade?"
"Yeah, I know 'em, I 'ad them vests and pants off 'er. Fuckin' shop rotten they were."
"Well, Mrs Goodman asked our Tony if he knew a gell ter werk Saturdays."
"Twelve an' six she charged me for 'em, bleedin' rob dog." I thought I had better get quickly to the point.
"She's payin' ten bob a week."
"I wish I'd 'ad 'em off ole Taffy now, at least 'e ... how much?"
"Ten bob Mom, fer werkin nine 'til six an' I gorra go an' see 'er Monday if I wanna do it, our Tony ses." Mom considered for a moment.

"Well, goo an' see 'er then if ya want." So far, so good. It had not been as difficult as I thought. But Mom had one stipulation and she pointed the bread knife at me for emphasis. "You jus' mek sure 'ow much she's gonna pay ya, that's all."

I had often spent time looking in Goodman's shop window at the plastic legs with their sheer nylon stockings, the thighs modestly covered by colourful head scarves. I had looked enviously at the shiny rolls of hair ribbon, the spotless white ankle socks and the boxes of plastic hair slides. Headless torsos displayed the latest in silky blouses and dainty hats, some with feathers stood on metal stands. On that Monday night when I walked into the shop, Mrs Goodman had put on the gold rimmed glasses that she wore on a chain around her neck. She was a small dark lady, and to me her speech and mannerisms seemed very foreign, but she had a placid disposition and never seemed to get upset about anything. She told me that the job would not involve serving in the shop, but making tea, carrying boxes of stock up and down the stairs, taking her pet Pekinese dog for walks and cleaning. I had good experience of that.

She wanted me to work one hour each night after school, from five until six, when the shop closed, and all day on Saturday. The wage was still only ten shillings. [50p] Ten shillings for about fourteen hours work seems very little now, but in 1957 it seemed a lot of money. It could buy me trips to the pictures, the ice rink, the baths, sweets every day, bus trips to Birmingham, lots of real hair ribbons, and still leave enough for a fish and chip supper every night. Well, something like that anyway.

Mrs Goodman asked me if I could start work the following night and I said 'Yes please'. There was one small snag. You had to be 12 to work part time and I was only 11 3/4. But Mrs Goodman was not unduly bothered and waved her spectacles dismissively.

"Ach, if anybody should ask you, say you are twelve and a half." Things were getting better all the time. I had got the job, was going to earn ten whole shillings a week and I must really look 12 1/2. Now there was only Mom to convince.

To my surprise, Mom readily agreed that I could start at Goodman's the following day after school. Then she turned to me and said

"Well now ya can start givin' me summat for ya keep, can't ya?"

What she meant was that I had to give her half my wages towards housekeeping, just as if I had started working full time. She had made the same stipulation when Tony had got his job so I could not complain, and anyway, five bob [25p] was better than nothing. But then Mom had another thought.

"An' don't forget, ya gorra do ya werk 'ere afore ya goo over there." As if I could forget.

On Tuesday night I raced home from school, bolted my jam sandwich, ran some errands to the shop, filled the coal bucket, did the washing up and set off for Goodman's Haberdashery shop. I had no way of knowing it, but my little part time job would open up a new world for me, a world I did not think existed except on the pictures. I discovered that there was a different sort of life from the one we lived in Nelson Street, and I discovered something about that life I had never even suspected.

As Mrs Goodman had said, my duties were cleaning, tidying, making the tea and generally being useful around the shop. On Saturdays I also had to take her Pekinese dog for walks. He was called, of all names, Tony, and that is probably why I took an instant dislike to him. He was fat and lazy with a squashed in face and he made a funny noise when he breathed. He did not seem to like exercise very much, so our walks would usually get no further than Nelson Street for a cup of tea with Mom. Mrs Goodman had told me that one of her cleaners had once hit Tony with a broom, and since then he had attacked all brooms on sight. At home I would shove our old yard broom into Tony's face driving him into fits of fury. If he did not get his exercise walking, then he certainly got it fighting our broom.

Mr Goodman was as small, dark and placid as his wife and never said very much at all. He was not in the shop very often because he ran a stall in Smethwick Market four days a week, including Saturday. I soon came to an arrangement with Mr Goodman that I would stay over for half an hour on Saturday nights to help unload the market stock from his little green van. I would carry the dozens of white boxes of ribbon, elastic, socks, stockings and buttons, upstairs to the store room and Mr Goodman would give me an extra two shillings or sometimes even half a crown [10p or 12.5p]. I made sure that Mom never found out about this extra money or she would have demanded her cut.

Mr Goodman liked to smoke and could not seem to go long without one of his favourite Woodbines, but he was never allowed to smoke in the shop. One day Mrs Goodman had come in to find a lighted cigarette burning away on top of the old wooden cash till. When she went out now she would turn to me and say,

"Now Carole, Mister Goodman is not allowed to smoke in here. It is bad for him and one day he will set us all on fire."

She always referred to her husband as 'Mister Goodman', even when speaking directly to him. I was supposed to tell her if he had smoked in the shop while she was out, but as soon as the door closed behind her, Mister Goodman would pull out his packet of Woodbines, wink at me and put a nicotine stained finger to his lips. I would carry on with my work, pretending not to notice, and he would puff happily away. I never had the heart to tell on him, but I always brought in the bottle of Air Wick from the toilet for a few moments when his wife was due to return. I was sure that my extra two bob for unloading was partly hush money.

One of the first things I did when I started to work at the shop was to clean out the little back room they used as a kitchen. It looked as though it had not been touched for years, so I really went to town on it. I scrubbed the floor, washed down the walls and got years of grime off the old stone sink. I cleaned the tiny window so that light could get in again, and made some little pleated curtains out of sheets of old wrapping paper. I scrubbed the wooden table until the top shone white, I chipped the lumps of solid sugar out of the glass basin, and even managed to get the dark brown stains off the tea spoons. No one had told me to do this, but I had now reached a stage where, if I saw a mess, I cleaned it up almost without thinking.

The Goodmans were impressed by my apparent enthusiasm for cleaning and I was pleased that they were. It gave me an un-familiar good feeling inside, a feeling that all the cleaning at home never did. I worked in that little shop for nearly five years and can honestly say that I enjoyed every minute. True, the wages were not over generous, but the Goodmans were kind and considerate. They seemed interested in what I did and thought, a reaction that I had never experienced before from grown ups.

The Goodmans had a grown daughter called Jacqueline and I was very impressed when Mrs Goodman told me that she worked in London at the BBC. Jacqueline was small and dark like her

parents, but when I first saw her I was puzzled and disappointed.
I had expected to recognise her face or her voice because I
thought that everyone who worked for the BBC must be a perf-
ormer of some sort, or at least an announcer. I found out later
that she was a typist.

Jacqueline came back home from time to time and the Goodmans
always got very excited. I would be sent into Birmingham to fetch
Jacqueline's favourite confectionery from Kunzel's, the cake shop
in Victoria Square. This was a box of six 'special' chocolate eclairs
made with real cream that cost a shilling each [5p]. I never knew
such things existed only walking distance from Nelson Street, and
I had never known anybody who had special eclairs for their tea.
I could just imagine Mom's reply if I had asked her to get eclairs
from Kunzel's for our tea. As I walked back along the Parade, I
would hold the box so that passers by could see the big letter 'K'
printed in red on it, and they would know that I had been to the
poshest cake shop in town.

Jacqueline was always nice to me but I did not really look forward to her visits. I could not help but notice the love and
affection the little Jewish couple lavished on their only child.
Naturally, at these times, their interest in me declined and I
was childishly jealous. Her presence in the shop only served
to remind me how different was my own home life from hers,
and I was always relieved when Jacqueline went back to London.

I had once told Mrs Goodman that my favourite lessons at school
were drawing, painting and model making, and she had seen some
of my work. One day, out of the blue, she asked me if I would
like to dress the shop window because she was finding it more
difficult to climb in and out of the space behind the curtains.
Would I? I certainly would.

From then on window dressing became one of my jobs, in fact,
my favourite job. I spent hours crouching in the hot alcove
behind the plate glass arranging and re-arranging the dummy
legs, heads and torsos. The silky blouses I would pad out with
cotton wool at the front to emphasise the breasts, then nip in
the waists with pins at the back and add a shiny plastic waspie
belt. I would drape the latest flared and pleated skirts over the
nylon clad legs with layers of frothy white petticoats underneath.
Then I would lay out matching sets of skimpy underwear, brass-
ieres, knickers and suspender belts, in which I fondly imagined
were seductive patterns. At the front of the window went the
more down to earth school socks, hair ribbon, interlock vests

113

and pants for the older women. Sometimes at night I would
sneak back to the shop and admire my handywork in the lighted window, comparing it with the displays in other shops
along The Parade. Mine was always the best, I thought. In
any event, the first time I did the window for the January
sale, Mrs Goodman told me

"Carole I have sold more than ever this year, I am sure it must be
your window that has done it." Maybe she was just being kind, but
her words gave me a great boost, a feeling of pride and worth that
I had never experienced until then.

Soon I could not imagine life without the daily stint at Goodman's
Haberdashery or my Saturdays spent making cups of tea, stacking
boxes and walking the reluctant Tony round to Mom's. And I could
not imagine life without my seven and sixpence wages either. Mom
had made it clear that she expected me to buy my own underwear,
socks, ribbons and so on, now that I was earning 'good money'.
But I did not mind this at all, for at least I had the freedom to
choose what I bought, within reason. Even when I reached 13
and was taking a lot more interest in what I wore, some of Mrs
Goodman's blouses were still a bit too 'off the shoulder' for
me. And I certainly did not dare to take home a pair of those
nylons with black diamonds up the legs. Make up was also out
of the question because Mom had told me that Dad would 'slap
it off my face' if he ever caught me wearing any.

I opened my own clothing account with Mrs Goodman and would
go through the new stock each week like the Revenge of Dracula,
putting aside anything I fancied for myself. Mrs Goodman gave
me a card and let me pay a shilling [5p] a week out of my wages
off the bill. This was something else I did not tell Mom about
because I knew she would say I was too young to be starting
'knock'. Knock was only for old married women like Mom and
Liza Hunt.

I had been working at the Goodman's shop for two happy years
when something happened that forced me to take a critical look
at the way we lived at 29 Nelson Street. Until then I had assumed
that my life would always be bound up in that rabbit warren of
grimy factories and run down houses called Ladywood. It came
as a shock when I saw another way of life.

One quiet Saturday afternoon in November, I was making tea in
the shop kitchen when Mrs Goodman came in. This was unusual
because she rarely left the shop and the till unattended. She
seemed to have something on her mind.

"Carole, I have got a problem." She began chewing on the arm of her spectacles. For a moment I was terrified that she was going to say she could not afford to pay me any more and I would have to leave. But she went on,

"My house maid is having a baby soon and cannot work. We are having Jacqueline home and some friends and relatives to stay, and I think that it will all be too much for me and Mister Goodman "

My head swam as I listened. A maid? I had never heard anything about a maid before. The Goodmans had once lived in the rooms above the shop, but as their business prospered they had bought a house in the Moseley area of Birmingham. I knew they had a man to do the gardening and a lady came in to clean, but now a maid? What sort of house did they live in? Only people on the pictures had maids.

"I was wondering if your mother would let you come and stay with us for a few days over the holiday (she mentioned some religious festival) to help me in the house and with the food. What do you think?"

I thought it would be great. A few days away from Nelson Street, the chores and the kids and the rows. True, I would be taking the place of Mrs Goodman's maid, but it was still a big step up from being a skivvy. I could hardly wait to get home that night and ask Mom about it. I hoped for the best but was prepared for the worst.

Mom listened patiently as I blurted out my story, interrupting me only the once.

"Maid? She's gorra fuckin' maid then?"
"Yes Mom."
"Well, fuck me." As to could I go or not, "You'd better ask ya Dad".

"Maid? She's gorra fuckin' maid then?", was Dad's only comment apart from, "Well, if ya Mom ses it's all right." I took that as a definite 'yes'.

Even so, I could hardly believe it when a few days later, I found myself in Albert Street in the City centre, waiting for the bus that would take me to Moseley and Mrs Goodman's. I had two carrier bags of things I thought I might need during my three day stay. I knew that maids wore a uniform, so I had packed

the cookery apron and hat that I had made at school. It
was a Friday afternoon and the shop was to be closed from
then until the following Tuesday morning while the Goodmans
entertained about a dozen of their closest friends and relatives.

I had the conductor put me off the bus at Augusta Road where I
saw the small dark figure of Mrs Goodman. She seemed relieved
that I had got there, and as we walked the short distance to the
house I could not help noticing the size and elegance of the prop-
erties that lined the road. Some of the front gardens were so big
we could not even see the house. Mrs Goodman had bought Tony
on his lead, and even he seemed quite pleased to see me on his
home ground.

We turned in at an imposing gateway and crunched along a wide
drive. I began to wonder if we would ever reach the front door,
but when I saw the house I felt something akin to fright. It was
so big, so high, so so massive. I was not going to stay in there
surely, not me, Carole Biddle from Nelson Street.

As we got near, the front door was opened by Mr Goodman,
who looked even smaller than usual in that massive doorway.
He gave a mock bow and ushered me into the hall.

"Welcome to our home, Carole.", he said.

I stumbled inside clutching my carrier bags, and my face must
have been a picture as I gaped around. A wide staircase of dark
polished wood curved down into the vast space they called 'the
front hall'. The only other time I had seen such a staircase,
Nelson Eddy and Jeanette McDonald had been singing a duet
on it. At the bottom was a sparkling glass chandelier with
dozens of bulbs shaped like candles.

I felt like crying. So it was all true after all. People really
did live like this, it was not just an invention of the people
who made films. And the smell. A heady scent that made me
feel giddy, which I later discovered was lavender furniture
polish. No cooking, no piss, no bleach, no onions, just polish.

"Well, what do you think then?" Mr Goodman's voice brought
me back to my senses.

"It's it's", but I could not find the right words. His wife must
have seen my confusion and took charge.
"Leave her alone now Mister Goodman. Come with me Carole
and I'll show you to your room."

116

I followed her up the staircase in a trance. Show me to my room. It was just like being in a hotel, not that I had ever been in one, but it could not be better than this. Upstairs there were more wonders. The bath had a room all to itself and the water ran hot night and day. The lavatory was actually inside the house, and it was white and sparkling. There were toilet rolls, not cut up squares of last week's *Sunday Pictorial*. I was to sleep in Jacqueline's old room, and as I stood staring at the fitted wardrobes, the full length mirror and the kidney shaped dressing table, I realised with a shock that tonight, for the first time in my life, I would not have to share a bed with anybody. Later on, as I slid down between those spotless sheets, I found that Mrs Goodman had put in a little hot water bottle. I cried into the soft white pillow until I fell asleep.

The other people who stayed at the house on that long weekend were another revelation to me. Jacqueline I already knew, she was always kind to me, but the other middle aged guests were just as nice. They called me 'Carole' and never tried to embarrass me or make fun of my thick Brummie accent, although they must have been well aware that I was a fish out of water in that house. I met Mrs Goodman's elder brother, the interestingly named 'Mr Rich'. He was a big man with an intimidating black beard, but he went out of his way to be pleasant to the scared little girl who brought him his early morning tea. I did not even need my school cookery uniform.

"There is no need for dressing up Carole, you will be just like one of the family" Mrs Goodman had told me. Me, one of the family? If only ..

During that whole weekend no one got drunk or shouted or swore, there were no rows or punch ups and I never heard the work 'fuck', in any tense. It was wonderful but it was also a shock. I thought of my own home with its smells, slop pails, candles and cockroaches, and at last I understood what Dad meant when he said to Mom, 'Nance, we gorra get out of this fuckin' 'ole.' He knew, and now I knew, what people meant when they used the word slum. I had heard that word but had never made the connection with our home in Ladywood. Well, now I knew. My home was a slum and I was a slum kid. I felt deeply ashamed and was thankful that the Goodmans had never seen the inside of 29 Nelson Street and, if I had anything to do with it, they never would.

My short stay in that other world thrilled, shocked and depressed me. There was a popular song that went - *How they gonna keep her, down on the farm, after she's seen Paree?'* Now I had seen the 'Paree' of the Goodman's lifestyle, how could I ever go back to the farm of Nelson Street? Go back I must, but the seeds of discontent had been sown and nothing would ever be the same again.

At home I soon fell back into the routine of chores, school, church and work at the shop. I did not say much to Mom and Dad about my stay at Augusta Road, what was the point? They must have known how other people lived, that's why Dad went on about getting out of Ladywood some day. There seemed to be no chance of that at present, but fate is a funny thing, and although I did not have any inkling of it, our days at Nelson Street were numbered.

One Saturday morning I went to the shop as usual and found Mrs Goodman looking pale and drawn. She greeted me with a very soft,

"Good morning Carole". Something was wrong, and fearing it was something I had done, or not done, I went through to the kitchen to make some tea. As I filled the kettle at the sink I noticed that Tony's dog basket had gone from its usual place under the table. Nor was there any sign of Tony himself, and this was very unusual because he always came to the shop with the Goodmans in their little green van. I went back into the shop to ask about Tony but as soon as she saw me Mrs Goodman answered my unspoken question.

"Oh Carole, he was getting so old, he just couldn't get up anymore. Mister Goodman had to take him."

I knew at once what she was avoiding putting into words. Tony was dead. He had been put down. I knew all about death, I had been around it often enough, and Tony was only a dog - a fat, spoiled lazy thing and not a proper dog at all. I could see that Mrs Goodman was getting upset, so I turned back into the kitchen. All right, it was a pity that Tony would never again waddle round with me to lap tea at Mom's or spend a happy hour attacking our yard broom, but what did I care anyway? Then I caught sight of his lead and tiny collar hanging forlornly on the hook above where his basket had been, and I broke down. I cried and cried until Mrs Goodman started to cry. In the end she had to send me home for the day, I was crying so much.

Mom was drinking tea at the kitchen table when I walked in, tears streaming down my face, and she looked up in surprise.

"What the bloody 'ell's wrung wi you then?", she demanded. I could hardly speak for sobbing.

"It's.. it's T.. T Tony." Mom looked concerned.

"Well, what's 'appened then?" she asked.

"He .. he .. he's dead.", I finally managed to blurt out. Mom shot up from her chair, her cup and saucer crashing to the floor.

"Dead. Dead. What the fuckin' 'ell ya mean, dead?", she yelled, a rising note of panic in her voice. I wondered why Mom was getting so excited. Yes, she had let Tony drink tea from her saucer but surely she was not that fond of him? Then I realised what she was thinking.

"No Mom. Not our Tony. Mrs Goodman's Tony, Tony the dog." Mom slumped back in her chair.

"Oh my God ..... the fuckin' dog. You nearly give me 'art attack ya daft bugger." But she was too relieved to be really angry.

1. Saturday night at the Nelson, Mom and Dad in their favourite Smoke Room seats, c 1958.

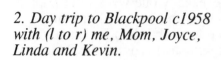

2. Day trip to Blackpool c1958 with (l to r) me, Mom, Joyce, Linda and Kevin.

When Nelson Got his Eye Back

Over the years, Mom had built up quite a collection of catch
phrases, put downs and smart answers to deal with the many and
awkward questions we asked her. When we were little it was easy;

"Mom, can I 'ave a bike?"
"Yeah, 'course ya can, wait 'til I've washed me 'ands."
"Eh?"
"You 'eard, wait 'til I've washed me 'ands."

I spent many impatient hours in our kitchen waiting for that
moment that never came. But she had plenty of other replies,
and as we got older and the questions more complicated,
so did the answers.

"Mom, why can't we 'ave a bigger 'ouse an' all 'ave our own
rooms?"
"Bigger 'ouses is bigger rents."
"But why Mom?"
"'Cause yer uncle ain't yer aunt and yer aunt ain't yer uncle,
that's why."

That line usually signalled the end of the discussion. Then there
was was my all time favourite. After my experiences at Augusta
Road I started to pester Mom about just when we might be moving
away from Ladywood, just like Dad had been talking about.

"Mom, when are we gonna get a new 'ouse like the ones by the
Rezza, with a gardin' an' everythin'?" [Rotton Park Reservoir]
"When? I can tell ya when all right."
"Go on then Mom. When? When?"
"When Nelson get's his eye back, that's when."

There was no answer to that, but completely out of the blue,
Nelson did get his eye back. It was exactly one week after poor
Tony (the dog) had been called to fight that big yard broom in
the sky. On Saturdays I came home from the shop for dinner
as I did from school, and it was raining as I crossed the Parade
and ran along Nelson Street. Down the entry and in through the
kitchen door I went, but there was no smell of dinner cooking,
no pans on the stove and no sign of Mom or the other kids.
Then I heard a muffled shout from the front room. It was
Mom's voice and I knew there was some crisis in progress.

120

"Carole. Is that you? C'mere quick."

I opened the front room door and saw Mom standing, staring at the ceiling. She was covered in white powder. There was white stuff all over the furniture and large lumps of it on the lino. I followed Mom's gaze and was horrified to see a gaping and ragged hole in the ceiling. Part of the floor of Mom and Dad's bedroom had collapsed and what was left tilted down towards us at a crazy angle.

"Thank Christ you've come, the bloody lot's fell in. I bin standin' 'ere for fuckin' ages." Mom gasped, without taking her eyes off the hole. I wondered why, but as I moved further into the room I could see the small figure of our Kevin in the bedroom above. He was sitting on an old metal bucket that served as his potty and was very close to the edge of the precipice. But he was calm and smiling and seemed fascinated by the fact that he could now look down into the front room without leaving the bedroom.

"Can't fuckin' move in case 'e falls. You goo up an' I'll stay 'ere an' catch 'im if the rest comes down.", Mom told me.

Just how she would catch Kevin, a hefty 2 year old, I did not know, especially if we were still attached to his bucket, It would not have been so bad if we had got him a proper plastic potty.

Upstairs I could see that Kevin would not sit still for very much longer, but as soon as I took a step into the room the whole floor shook, sending another shower of plaster dust down onto Mom's upturned face.

"Fer fucks sake be careful or you'll both come through.", she screamed.

Kevin still seemed to be enjoying this new game. He pointed at the gaping hole in the floor, smiled and gurgled,

"S'broke."

I did not give myself any time to think about what I was going to do, but reached out as far as I could, grabbed Kevin by the back of his shirt and yanked him off the bucket and out of the room. As I did so, that part of the floor and the bucket went crashing down into the front room. Luckily, Mom dodged out of the way in time.

This then, was the beginning of the unexpected end of our years at number 29 Nelson Street. Council workmen took one look and condemned the house as unfit for human habitation, but it was another two weeks before we were offered another house, during which Mom and Dad slept on the front room floor.

To Joyce and Linda and me, it seemed that our wildest dreams were about to come true. Nelson really was going to get his eye back. What would our new home be like, we wondered? Would we have our own rooms? Would the lavatory be inside the house? Would there be hot running water and perhaps even a garden.? We could not wait to find out.

One dinnertime when we came home from school, there was a new bunch of keys lying on the kitchen table with a little tag attached. Our new address. Then we all came down to earth with a bump, because the writing on the tag told us we would be moving to 33 Alexander Street, just two hundred yards from where we were. We were swapping our two up, two down and an attic for a three up, three down and an attic, so we would have a bit more living space, but still not an inside lavatory or bathroom and certainly no garden. Our back kitchen door in Alexander Street opened onto a communal yard just like the one in Nelson Street. All we needed now, I thought, was Liza Hunt effing and blinding around the yard to make the picture complete.

Up in the World

Our move to Alexandra Street after the collapse of the floor at Nelson Street coincided with a definite improvement in the Biddle family fortunes. Dad's business was still based at his ramshackle factory in Edward Street, but now our Tony had left school and was working for him, or rather with him, as Tony would always point out. Dad was also employing several more men to take on the extra work he was now getting. He was even talking about having a telephone installed at home, but the major event at that time was Dad's purchase of his first car. For Dad, it was an important step on his long journey to get out of 'this fuckin' hole', as he called Ladywood.

Very few people we knew owned a car, for most families it was an undreamed of luxury. Dad getting one came about through

a family we knew called Grove, who lived in Edward Street close
to Dad's factory. Our Joyce was friendly with their eldest girl,
Carol, who was in her class at school, and she often brought her
to our house in Alexandra Street. But the Grove's were known
locally as a rough family and certainly not very honest. We knew
this because Dad often bought metal working tools from Mr Grove
that had fallen off the back of a lorry, just like our TV set.
and we had other reasons to mistrust the Groves.

For their wedding anniversary one year, Dad had bought Mom
a 'gold' wrist watch from a mail order advertisement in the
Daily Mirror. Mom prized this watch above all other things and
hardly ever took it off, except when she washed her hands in the
kitchen sink. One night as they were getting ready to go to the
Nelson, Mom noticed that she was not wearing her beloved watch.
It was not by the side of the sink where she usually put it while
washing. She called Dad, but he had not seen it either. We all
helped her search the house from top to bottom, even the outside
lavatories, but there was no sign of the watch. Mom sat deep in
thought for a few moments then suddenly turned to Joyce.

"'Ere, you 'ad that Carol Grove round 'ere this mornin', didn't
ya?"
"Yes Mom", Joyce whispered, then for some unknown reason
she began to cry. But Mom knew.
"C'mon Alf, I've gorra feelin' about this, we'll goo round ter
them fuckin' Groves. "

Grimly determined, round they went. While they were away,
Joyce sat snivelling to herself and I could not get out of her
what was wrong. When they came back Mom was triumphantly
wearing her watch. Just what happened round at the Grove's I
never found out, but Mom was happy again, pausing only to
give our Joyce a few slaps around the face before setting off
for the pub. Joyce's friendship with Carol Grove survived
this, but she never brought her to the house again.

It was the same Carol Grove who had got Joyce a belting a
couple of years earlier, after which she had been given the
family nickname of 'the dope'. You see, Joyce could sometimes be, putting it bluntly, very thick. It would have been
kinder to say 'naive', but we did not know that word then.

Carol Grove, who was a couple of years older than Joyce,
took her into the city centre one Saturday morning to visit
Woolworth's in New Street. Joyce came safely back and told

123

us about all the lovely things she had seen in Woolworth's and
the other big shops. Then, as Mom was about to dish up the
dinner, Joyce went up the yard to the lavatory. None of us
thought anything of this except Mom who, as soon as Joyce
came back, went up there herself.

We were all sitting around the table when Mom came back in
and we saw she was holding something. Down on the table she
put two handfuls of cheap jewellery, rings, bracelets, a neck-
lace, some pairs of earrings and other bits. She stood there with
arms folded over her pinnie as we all stared in amazement at the
little pile. After a few moments and without another word, Mom
pushed the pile of jewellery directly in front of Joyce. She
looked at the pile, then up at Mom, then back at the pile, and
burst into tears.

Don't ask me how Mom knew, but she did. She soon had the
full story out of Joyce, about how Carol Grove had told her
that it was a special free day at Woolworth's and you could
have what you liked without paying for it. And our Joyce had
believed her.

After our experience of the Grove family it was a surprise when
Dad announced that he had bought a second hand car off Mr
Grove. We could hardly believe that our Dad had forked out the
huge amount of £10 for a battered old car. But my Dad was not
daft, he had bought it on the understanding that Mr Grove would
teach him to drive as part of the deal. Needless to say, Mom was
not too pleased when she found out where the car had come from.

"You'd berra clean them fuckin' seats if yer want me to gerrin
it after 'er fat arse 'as bin on 'em." She was referring to Mrs
Grove, who was a large woman. But Dad was obviously thrilled
with his first motor car and just couldn't wait to start driving.

One Sunday morning, he offered to take us all for a spin in the
country. Mom refused to go, reminding him that he had not yet
passed his test. Dad would not be put off, so Joyce, Linda and
me clambered excitedly in and onto the black and shiny rear seat.
Mom came to the front door and saw us off with the warning,

"You'll kill yerselves drivin' round in that thing.", but after
much gear grinding and a few backfires, we pulled away. We all
leaned over Dad's shoulder as the speedometer needle crept up to
30 miles an hour and we left Ladywood behind. The horn had a
lovely throaty sound, like a duck with tonsillitis, and we kept

urging Dad to press the flat button on the steering wheel so we could hear it.

We were all thrilled with this unexpected trip into the country-side around Barr Beacon, and it all went well until we came to a narrow lane with a ford through a stream. The car stalled in the middle with water up to the running boards. Juggle with the controls and swear as he might, Dad could not get it to start. In the end we all had to get out and push, with the water nearly up to our knees. Once clear of the water, Dad used the starting handle and we made our way back home. When we pulled up outside our house Dad turned round to us and said,

"You lot gerrin an' change yer shoes an' socks - an' don't tell ya Mom what 'appened , you 'ear?"

"Yes Dad," we chorused and squelched down the entry. It proved something that I had suspected for a long time, even Dad was frightened of Mom.

Another sign that we were going up in the world was that most of the families we came across now were a lot worse off than us. The Kings were one such, and a more inappropriately named lot it would have been hard to imagine. They were the most downtrodden, deprived, depressed, hard up family that we had ever known, and we had known quite a few. The Kings and their ten children lived in a two up, two down and an attic at the top end of our yard in Alexandra Street, and compared to them our situation was like Hollywood.

The Kings were on National Assistance because Mr King had some illness which prevented him from working. 'Too fuckin' exhausted', Dad said. But the illness did not seem to prevent him from staggering down to the pub most nights. Mr King was a small man with a stooping walk and long, hairy arms that seemed to dangle past his knees. His chin jutted out and he had a very low forehead, dark hair almost meeting his bushy eyebrows. I did not know the word 'neanderthal' then, but on the wall of our classroom there was a picture of a cave-man and his family squatting around a fire which reminded me irresistibly of the Kings.

Unfortunately for the Kings' ten children, they had inherited their father's distinctive looks, boys and girls alike. To see them all milling around in the yard supervised by their father, while waiting for mother to hand out doorstep slices of bread

and scrape from the kitchen door, could be quite unnerving.
Mrs King was a thin, pale woman with sharp features who might
have been pretty at one time, but none of this had been passed
on to her offspring. As they were about the same age, in their
mid thirties, she and Mom got quite friendly.

It started one Monday dinner time when Mom was scraping
the remnants from our stew into one of the bins at the top
of the yard. Mrs King saw what she was doing and came hesit-
antly over.

"S'cuse me, but are you throwin' all that away?", she asked shyly.
"Yes love, it's only what the kids 'ave left on their plates."
"Well, I'll 'ave it off yer, if yer don't mind, it'll do for some
of me kids to 'ave."

Mom was a bit taken aback that there was anybody desperate
enough to want our leftovers, but she handed it over. Then
Mrs King told her that both gas and electricity had been cut off
for not paying the bills, and they had had no hot meals for weeks.
From then on Mom saved all our food scraps for the Kings, warning
us if we were slow to eat our dinners, 'C'mon, if ya don't wannit
the Kings'll 'ave it an' be glad.' Mom also started to pass on our
old clothes and other bits and pieces to Mrs King, who was always
pathetically grateful.

It was about this time that Dad passed his driving test and
started to take us on weekend camping trips to a site by the river
Severn at Stourport. We slept in a big canvas bell tent that our
Tony bought from old man Clements' junk shop. The old wind
up gramophone came along with Tony's pop records and we had
a great time. Telly, car and now holidays. Before we went, Mom
would give Mrs King a half crown to keep an eye on the house
and she would wave us off from the kerb, tears streaming down
her face as though she never expected to see us all again.
Dad was more cynical.

"Huh, no more of our stew fer a bit, that's why she's cryin'.",
he once commented as we pulled away. But Mom always maint-
ained that Mrs King was 'a decent sort' and her problems were
caused by her husband being unable, or more likely unwilling,
to go to work, and she was probably right.

It was lucky for the Kings that we had moved into the yard at
that time. Dad's business was doing well and money was not as

tight for us as it had been. Mom was now able to help out Mrs King and the kids in lots of little ways, but Dad had no time for them, especially Mr King. 'He's an idle bastard, 'e can't feed 'is kids but 'e can drink in the fuckin' Bell every night.' Dad was not daft, he knew the score, but as winter approached, Mom tackled him about giving Mrs King the money to pay her electricity bill.

"Oh Alf, all them kids an' no fire an' no 'ot dinners." Dad's reply was as short as it was expected.
"If he can't look after 'em, he shouldn't 'ave 'em, should 'e?"

But if Mom put her mind to it she could persuade Dad to do anything she wanted, and she certainly seemed to have developed a soft spot for the Kings. Perhaps she saw herself in Mrs King's predicament if she had gone on having kids and if Dad had not been a worker. Anyway, after a lot of talk, Dad finally agreed to help out the Kings 'just this once'. But he was not rash enough to hand over any cash. 'It'll be in the till at the Bell afore the night's out.' So it was Mom who took the money down to the Electricity Board showroom and the Kings got their supply reconnected. Mrs King was tearfully grateful, while her husband continued to drink in the Bell most nights.

The story does not have a happy ending and turned out as Dad had predicted, 'a bloody waste of time'. Within three months the King's electric supply was cut off again, and within two years there were two more mouths to feed in the King household. At least it proved that Mr King could not have been completely idle.

While the Kings's name was wildly inappropriate, the Roe family were aptly named. By the time she was 30 years old Mrs Roe had spawned fifteen children. My younger sister Linda was friendly with one of the Roe girls, Ginny, and she spent much of her free time at their terraced house in King Edward Road. We knew from what our Linda had told us, that the Roe family were a lot worse off than us; they would be with fifteen kids to feed. But I did not realise the true horror of their situation until one Saturday dinner time. The fact that Linda was always round there when Mom wanted her for some errand began to get on her nerves, so as she was dishing up the dinner on this particular Saturday Mom turned to me and said,

"I dunno what the fuckin' attraction is fer Linda at them Roe's. Goo round an tell 'er to come 'ome fer 'er dinner."

As I approached the Roe's house in King Edward's Road, I noticed that there were no curtains on the windows, upstairs or down. Always a bad sign this. I went down the entry and came into a bare yard. No curtains at the back either. The door was open, and just as I was going inside a little lad of about three, dressed only in his vest, ran past me into the house. I asked him if he knew where Linda might be and he called over his shoulder,

"In the kichin."

His bare bum disappeared in the direction of cooking smells and the sound of excited chatter. I followed him along the dingy passage until I found myself at the end of a line of Roe children, from tots to teenagers. They were screaming, shouting, fighting and jostling for position in the queue. Each of them had some sort of receptacle clutched in their hands. There were dinner plates, pudding basins, plastic dishes and even the odd metal cake tin. The line stretched around the corner and into a room I took to be the kitchen. I could not get past this struggling throng, so I had to wait patiently as the queue moved slowly forward. At last we reached the kitchen door and I could see into the room, and I will never forget what I saw.

The room was bare of furniture except for an ancient gas stove and a small wooden table. On the stove a blackened saucepan simmered a mixture of potatoes, gravy and onions. The bare floorboards were littered with piles of dirty nappies and overflowing receptacles that served as babies potties. There were metal buckets, an old paint tin, a crock pastry bowl and an old saucepan. The stone sink was full of nappies soaking in bleach and water, while the draining board was piled high with dirty plates and pans from previous feeding times. I was well used to bad smells, but the stench here hit me like a blow in the stomach and I felt myself heaving.

In the middle of all this, behind the table, stood Mrs Roe, Ginny Roe and Linda. She was smiling happily, playing Lady Bountiful ladling out the kid's dinners. Years later when I saw the film *Oliver Twist* the scenes in Fagin's kitchen reminded me of the Roe's. So this was the attraction for our Linda. As soon as each kid had its plate filled with the brown stuff, they would dash away in search of somewhere to sit and eat. There were no chairs so they took window ledges, stairs, front and back steps. Even the communal lavatory block outside was occupied by scoffing kids. It was the worst thing I had ever seen. The Roes seemed to have abandoned all pretence of respectability and were living from one round of grub to the next. We found out later that the grocer a few doors away felt sorry for them and sent in scraps of food such as cabbage leaves, soft potatoes, spoiled fruit and even potato peelings.

At last I managed to drag Linda away and report to Mom what I had seen. She forbade Linda to go round to the Roe's again saying 'You dunno what yer might get.' She was more right than she knew, because it was not long before Ginny Roe had two babies of her own, fathers unknown. She was 15 years old when the second was born. Some time later we heard that Mrs Roe had been sterilised by order of the Health Department.

"I like riding in my car..."

When our Tony was 15 he left school and went to work for Dad at his factory in Edward Street. Dad and Tony never got on very well as father and son, so you can imagine what their relationship was like as boss and worker. The trouble was that Tony knew everything that there was to know, or so he thought, and did not like anyone telling him differently. He and Dad were forever falling out over something at work (and at home), and Tony often threatened to give his notice and get a job at another local factory. "Any factory where Dad isn't the boss.", he would say.

It all came to a head one dinnertime, I was in the front room with Mom helping her put up the wages for Dad to pay out on the following Friday, when Dad walked in. He was in his usual bad mood and threw a set of National Insurance cards onto the table.

"You can mek 'is munney up Nance, 'e's fuckin' gooin'."

This was not unusual. Dad was always sacking someone, often saying, 'If I've gorra werk on fuckin' Sunday, then 'e's gorra fuckin' werk on Sunday or 'e can sling 'is 'ook.', and that would be it, no appeals, no second chances, the sack. But this time, when Mom looked at the cards that Dad had flung down, she saw that they belonged to our Tony.

"What you gimme these for then, Alf?", she asked.

"Fuckin' Tony. Ses he can gerra job anywhere, so let 'im fuckin' try."

"Oh 'e don't mean it Alf, it's all talk with 'im." Mom always took Tony's side in these disputes.

"Well, I'm fuckin' sick of 'im gooin' on about how 'ard done by 'e is. He can goo, if that's what 'e wants."

Dad was not prepared to argue about it, so Mom duly made up Tony's money with holiday pay owed and pinned the packet to his cards. Then she put it alongside his place at the dinner table.

Tony came in, sat down and ate his dinner, hardly glancing at the packet and cards. We were all waiting to see what he would do but he was giving no hints. With dinner finished, Dad went back to the factory without speaking to Tony while Mom and me watched him from the front room as he sat fingering the packet. It was decision time. Back to the factory and Dad, or down the road to another job? At last Tony got up, came into the front room and threw down his cards and pay packet in front of Mom. Without a word he turned and walked out.

"Y'see, I knew it was all talk.", said Mom with some satisfaction.

He hadn't got the guts, I thought with equal satisfaction. When my time came to assert my independence, I would have the guts, I promised myself. But guts or no, Tony knew which side his bread was buttered, and as it turned out he had made the right decision.

As soon as he started earning, Tony had got rid of his old bike and bought a motor bike and side car. This contraption was not very glamorous or with it, but at least he could take his girl friend out with no danger of falling off, something he often did from his push bike. But there were snags with this arrangement. In winter Tony's girl friend, Mary, would be warm and snug in the sidecar while Tony was left exposed to the elements. When they came home, Tony would often be walking stiffly, like a robot, his face white and frozen from the cold. So one day, at the end of a particularly bad winter, the combination was traded in for a car. When we heard about this, us kids were thrilled. Now we were a two car family, something almost unheard of. We must really be going up in the world.

We all wondered what sort of car it would be. A snappy, open top red sports model? Or one of new Ford Classics built along the lines of an American Cadillac? Tony always had big ideas, so maybe it would be a Jaguar. But when we first saw Tony driving down our street in his new car, we were puzzled. That wasn't a car surely? Not that shape? It looked more like a miniature version of one of the flying saucers people were claiming to see. And what a funny colour, bright blue, with a plastic dome on top and just three wheels.

A bubble car was a plastic shell with two small seats mounted over the engine, but our Tony seemed oblivious to any disadvantages and was thrilled to bits with it. Parked outside our front door, it soon attracted the attention of the local kids.

"Hey look at that. Fuckin' Martians 'ave landed."
"Berrit goos at 'undred."
"Huh, berrit don't."
"Warra poxy colour."
"Me Dad ses the Jerrys mek 'em, can't be no bleedin' good then."
"There ain't no doors on it. 'Ow do they gerrin?"
"Crawl under an' come up thru' the floor, you prat, what did yer think?"

When they started to kick the bubble car to test its strength, Tony came out and chased them off.

"Cheeky buggers, you'd think they'd never sin a decent car before."

Tony's girl friend, Mary, came from a large Irish family. Like many others, food was scarce in their house, so most nights Mary would come straight from work to have her tea with us. She too was thrilled with the bubble car and could not wait to go for a ride.

After we had had our tea, cooked meals for the workers, jam sandwiches for us kids, Tony would commence his pudding ritual. Every night he would buy, out of his own money, a special pudding for him and Mary. He would never give us kids any and took great delight in tormenting us with it. He would stand at the stove, boiling up a tin of steamed treacle duff and a saucepan of Birds custard. As he stirred the custard he glanced at us kids every now and then, the look on his face like that of a medieval torturer

131

At last he would flop the duff onto a big white plate then cover it with layers of thick custard. The smell from this delicious concoction made all our mouths water. Tony and Mary usually ate their pudding in the front room, and as he carried the plate through Tony would waft it temptingly under our noses, administering a sharp clout round the ear to any of us who dared to put out a finger. To Tony I suppose it was just a silly game of one upmanship over us, but today it is called aversion therapy and done under medical supervision. What we did not know as we watched the treacle pudding float past was on that very evening, fate had already planned to take him down a peg

At last Tony and Mary finished their pudding and, foregoing their usual snogging session, went out to the bubble car. We all trooped out after them to see them off. The street kids gathered again to watch the strange flying saucer thing take off from the kerb and move slowly down the street. They gave a loud cheer as it puttered away and then lost interest as it vanished around the corner. It was not raining, so Mom and the kids and me all stayed outside to see them come back. The minutes passed but there was no sign of the car. Tony had told us that he was only going around the block, so where were they?

More minutes dragged by until at last we saw them turn the corner again and head back towards us. But something was wrong. The car looked somehow different, it looked smaller. Yes, of course it did, there was only half of it there. As they got nearer, we could see that one side of the fibreglass body had been completely torn away. Somewhere around the block they had obviously come into violent contact with something bigger and tougher than the bubble car. As they pulled up, Mary and Tony's legs were plainly visible through the gaping hole. Tony was very pale and Mary was holding a bloodstained handkerchief to the side of her head. I looked quickly at Joyce and Linda, but Mom saw us and hissed,

"Don't you dare laugh, he'll fuckin' kill ya."

At this new sensation the street kids were back in force.

"Bleedin' Jerry car, it's fell apart."
"They've gorra door now."
"Where's the other 'arf, Tony?"
"'Ere, let's goo an' find it, Tony might give us summat."

They all set off in search of two or three square feet of blue fibre-glass lying somewhere around the block. Tony and Mary climbed shakily out of the remains and went quickly into the house. Mom waved frantically at the rest of us to stay outside and so avoid the risk of being murdered by Tony if he saw our laughter. He never had much of a sense of humour, my brother. But we were glad to obey because we could laugh as loud and long as we liked in the street, and we did. Thinking back, the sight of our Tony and Mary sitting grim faced in half a bubble car was well worth all those nights when we got no treacle pudding.

Tony and Mary at Blackpool at about the time of the bubble car disaster.

These Dangerous Years

Nineteen fifty eight saw me enter those awful years of limbo between becoming a teenager and leaving school, when we would at last be earning some money to back up our big ideas. I had passed the stage when Mom and Dad were all powerful and knew everything, but had reached a dangerous age when Mom and Dad were still all powerful but in my opinion, knew nothing. Pop music was here, changes were underway, but teenagers were not yet fully confirmed as a species in their own right. I had inherited Mom's determination and her temper. Tony had inherited Dad's ambition and need to be top dog in everything he tried, to be 'cock of the walk' as Mom put it. He was also earning, had money to spend and was at the 'I know everything' stage. Joyce, Linda and Kevin were still just babies, and when Mom and Dad were out there was always a violent conflict between me and Tony as to who actually ruled the roost.

I was now 13 and Tony two years older. I suppose all brothers and sisters fight, especially when their ages are so close, but our battles went far beyond what they now call sibling rivalry.

Tony was determined to assert his supposed authority and I was equally determined not to give in. Mom knew what was going on and would often warn Tony before they went out, 'You lay an 'and on 'er tonight and I'll fuckin; kill ya.' But these dire warnings had little effect on our Tony. Sooner or later during the evening he would lose his temper with me.

Tony was very friendly with a girl called Barbara Bennett. In the evenings, when Mom and Dad had left for the pub, and if me and the kids were playing outside, Tony and Barbara would have the kitchen to themselves for a heavy breathing session. One particular night, Joyce and Linda were playing in the yard and Tony was waiting impatiently for me to take our Kevin and join them. But I did not feel like going out, or rather, I did not feel like doing anything to please Tony.

"Why don't yer goo round ter Veronica's then?", he asked.

"'Cause I gorra look after 'im ain't I?" I told him, indicating our Kevin who was turning out the knife drawer, his favourite plaything.

"Well, yer can tek 'im with yer, can't yer?" Tony persisted.
"No. I ain't draggin' 'im round with me all night, an' I gorra get them ter bed soon an' all.", I said, nodding towards the yard where Joyce and Linda were screaming and shouting.

"Well, tek the fuckin' lorrof 'em with yer then." Tony was getting irritated now as Barbara would soon be clicking her way up the entry in her four inch stiletto heels.

"No. I ain't gonna drag that lot round with me, you prat."
"Don't you call me a prat."
"Well you are - PRAT!"
"Yer cheeky fucker." SLAP.
"Don't yer 'it me yer bastard."
"What did yer say?" SLAP.

"Ow. Yer bastard, bastard."
"Watch yer fuckin' mouth will ya."

And so it went on and on. As it happened, Barbara never turned
up that night, and by the time Mom and Dad came in from the
pub Tony had given up on her and gone to bed.

I was still attending Follet Osler School on and off, mostly off.
Upt to now I had never defied Mom or Dad and rarely answered
them back. It was always a painful experience if I did. But this
teenage thing was getting to me and Joyce and Linda sometimes
followed my lead. Usually we all got into trouble, and at 14 I
still was not too old to feel Dad's wrath.

It was a cold, dark winter's evening and Joyce, Linda and me
had just got back from school. We took up our usual positions
to thaw out in front of a roaring coal fire in the front room.
Mom was in the kitchen cooking tea for Dad and Tony. As
Tony was now earning he was entitled to a cooked meal and
could even order what he wanted. For the rest of us it was jam
sandwiches or a banana piece. Just then we heard Mom's voice
from the kitchen.

"We need some milk. 'Oo's goin' ter the shop fer me then'?"
The shop was about a hundred yards away from our front
door, but not one of us moved.
"Oh Mom, I've just took me shoes an' socks off.", was Joyce's
excuse.
"Oh Mom, I can't goo, it's snowin' an' me shoe's lerrin in.",
was Linda's.
"'Ere y'are then Carole, come an' get the munney.", I thought
fast.
"Oh Mom, I've gorra goo ter the shop ter werk in a minit, I
ain't gooin' out in this twice, I'll get bloody soaked."
There was a short, pregnant silence as we waited for Mom's
reaction, then her head appeared round the kitchen door.
"Right, fuck the lorra ya then, I'll goo me fuckin' self."

Before any of us could speak or move, Mom had struggled into her
coat and gone out, slamming the front door. We looked uncertainly
at each other. Perhaps one of us should have gone? Then I glanced
at the clock. Dad would be home soon. The slamming of the kitchen
door made us all jump. We prayed it was Mom, but Dad's head
appeared around the door.

135

"Where's yer Mom, then?" he asked pleasantly. No one spoke. There was just no way to convey the information Dad wanted, no way to tell him that Mom had gone out into the snow storm, to the shop, while we toasted ourselves in front of that roaring fire.

"I said, where's ya Mom gone?." Somebody had to answer him and I was the eldest.
"Gone to the shop" I whispered. Dad could not have reacted more violently if I had told him she had run off with the milkman.
"Gone to the fuckin' what?" He strode over to us as if he had not heard correctly.
"Gone to the shop fer a bottle of milk Dad." I had no option but to tell him. His eyes widened as he stared at the three of us, shivering in front of that blazing fire. Then he glanced out of the window where the snow was blowing wildly against the panes.
"An' why didn't you fuckin' go, eh?" he asked, his face only a foot or so away from mine.
"Don't know Dad," was all I could think of. Then the same quest-ion to Joyce and Linda and the same answer,
"Don't know Dad."

With one quick movement of his arm, Dad managed to slap us all hard across our faces in one go with a prolonged 'slaaarp' sound that echoed around the room. I had seen the Three Stooges do the very same thing with the same sound on the screen at the Lyric, but we did not laugh. Dad turned and went back into the kitchen. This time he had got nowhere near his fork before being called to action.

A short while later the front door opened and Mom came in clutching the bottle of milk. As she struggled out of her wet coat, she took in the scene at a glance. The three of us, standing there, holding the side of our faces and snivelling. I knew what she was thinking and Mom was never one to hide her thoughts.

"Serves ya fuckin' right."

Of Boys, Booze and Babbies

It was a Saturday night and I was 14 years old. Teenagers had happened, rock'n'roll was here to stay, but where was I? At the local hop, bopin' the night away? Pumping shilling pieces into the Motorola juke box with my friends in some coffee bar? Round at Veronica's trying on our new 'cross your heart' bra's? No. I was in my usual place at our kitchen sink and up to my armpits in dishwater. As I thought about the hundred and one other little jobs I had to do before Mom and Dad got back from the Nelson, I could hear the tinny sound of Neil Sedaka at full blast from our Tony's record player in the front room.

> 'Oh Carole, I am but a fool,
> I love you, though you treat me cruel.'

Would I ever get a chance to treat anybody cruel, I wondered, or ever be loved, come to that? But this was the regular Saturday night scene at our house in Alexander Street. Tony was holed up in the front room with his mates and a couple of local girls, laughing, dancing, snogging and heaven only knew what else while I slaved away in the kitchen.

Some nights, when one of the girls failed to turn up, Tony's mates would be in and out of the kitchen trying to lure me into the front room to make up the numbers. Their approach drowned by the blaring music, they would sneak up behind me and push their hands under my arms for a quick feel of my ever growing breasts. Or they would quietly lift my skirt to see what colour knickers I was wearing, or they would … well, you get the idea. Even at 14 I flattered myself that I had a good line in put downs to fend off these spotty Herberts.

"C'mon Carole, come an' 'ave a dance with us, will ya?", trying to grab my wet hands.
"Geroff. I'm fed up, not fuckin' 'ard up."
"Oh goo on - 'ole Alan's got nobody ter dance with", patting my bum.
"Well, lerrim dance with our Tony, I'll lend 'im a skirt if ya like."
"Can I 'elp ya wash up then?", grabbing me round the waist.
"No, fuck off will ya.", slapping the wet dish cloth around his face. And so it would go on, them pestering, me refusing and finally, they would lose interest.

137

Although I was never really that keen on rock'n'roll, I would
have liked to join in the laughing, dancing, singing and whatever else went on in our front room on Saturday night, especially
the whatever else. My chores were really just an excuse, for the
truth was that I was still terrified of having any soft of physical
contact with a boy. Despite being a mature 14 year old and living
where I did, what I knew about sex could have been written on a
pin head with a pneumatic drill.

Mom had given me stern warnings about the fate of girls who
let boys 'mess about' with them. I knew a lot of dirty jokes,
and I had heard the whispered conversations of older girls in the
lavatory at school. But I still knew nothing about the mechanics
of sex or baby making, or how I might indulge in the one without
getting caught for the other. For all I knew, it took just a crafty
fumble up the entry to find yourself pushing a pram nine months
later. But I knew that I would never find myself in that position
because Dad would kill me stone dead long before the pram stage.
And that was another hang up of mine, the fear of what Mom and
Dad might do to me if they found out I had been 'going' with boys,
whatever that might mean.

I was the eldest girl so I suppose I got the worst of it, but as
soon as I reached 12 and my periods started, Mom and Dad's
attitude towards me seemed to harden. Now it seemed, I was a
liability, I could bring home 'trouble', I could threaten the respectability of the Biddle household. All us girls had to go through
it. As our time of the month approached, Mom would keep an
even closer eye on us.

"'Ave yer come on yet?"
"No Mom."
"Yer fuckin' late, ain't you?"
"Yes Mom."
"Why's that then?"
"Don't know Mom."

Then she would give us what was known as an 'old fashioned
look', and we would feel guilty as hell about something. The
interrogation would be repeated the next day and until Mom got
the answer she wanted. Now I had reached that dangerous age,
my every move had to be accounted for and explained. Dad
was in some ways worse than Mom.

"Where you gooin', then?", as Dad noticed me moving towards
the kitchen door.
"Up the yard Dad."
"What fer?"
"To the lavvy."
"Well, don't be lung then."
"No Dad.", getting out of the door at last.
"An' bring that coal bucket in when ya come out the lav.", Dad's
voice echoed after me up the yard.

Mom and Dad had an obsession about me getting pregnant at an
early age and I could never understand why. Only when I had
a daughter of my own did I understand their anxieties. True,
there were some girls at school who had babies before they
left, but I was a virtual prisoner in my own home, so how
could whatever had to happen, happen to me? They seemed to
have decided to withhold any information that might prevent it
happening and, at the same time, prevent me from ever coming
into contact with members of the opposite gender. But by imposing even more restrictions on my movements they built up a
resentment which was to lead, within two short years, to a
break with them and Ladywood.

It was Mom who seemed to sense that there was trouble brewing,
and she did sometimes try to give me a little more freedom. Unfortunately, these efforts never seemed to work out as planned.
One night after Mom and Dad had come in from the pub, Mom
turned to me and said,

"'Ere, y'know the missus at the Nelson, Carol Pugh?"
"Yeah, warrabout 'er then?"
"Well, she wants somebody ter look after 'er babby on Saturday
night an' I told 'er that you'd do it." I must have looked
shocked because she went on,
"Oh she's gonna pay ya, don't worry."

But I was not worried, I would have done it for nothing just
to get out of the house for a bit. A whole Saturday night away
from that kitchen sink and the spotty Herberts, mixing with
normal people, in a pub. I could hardly believe it. But wait
a minute, I had almost forgotten, Mom and Dad would be right
there, all night, watching me. I might have known, freedom but
no freedom, Mom never missed a trick. However, baby sitting
under Mom and Dad's eyes was far better than washing up and
being touched up by Tony's mates. I decided to make the best
of it.

139

This was my big chance. Over the years I had been working
at Mrs Goodman's shop I had bought lots of teenage fashions,
most of which I had never had the chance to wear, and some that
I had not dared wear. Out came my flared rock'n'roll skirt with
three layers of white lace petticoats, my off the shoulder white
frilly blouse and my red plastic waspie belt. Black stockings and
stiletto heeled shoes would complete my ensemble. I took time
and much trouble getting ready for my baby sitting date, but when
I looked in the mirror I wondered if I had overdone it. Did that
black eye liner look all right with the blue eye shadow? Did my
lips look a bit too thick with that scarlet floss lipstick? And
was my off the shoulder blouse just a bit too off the shoulder?
No, I told myself, I was going to a pub and had to look at least
18. As for my blouse, I just had to remember not to bend forward
too much. And so, with my hair done in the popular pony tail I
clattered down the stairs on my four inch heels. Mom and Dad
had already left for the pub, but Tony was just coming in. He
took one look at me and burst out laughing.

"What the 'ell's that then?", he yelled. But I took it as a comp-
liment and set off for the Nelson.

All along the street I seemed to attract a lot of attention from
the local lads, with whistles, cat calls and shouts of 'Hey
Brigitte.' This last always used to worry me. I had been told
by some girls at school that I looked just like a French film
star who took her clothes off on screen, but I had never seen
any of her pictures, they were all 'X' certificate. I thought
that it might be some sort of joke and this 'Brigitte' was fat
or toothless or bald or something. I would never believe anybody who paid me compliments, and the most Mom and Dad
would say when I asked then how I looked was - 'all right'.

When I got to the pub the baby was safely asleep in his cot upstairs, so I decided to help out by taking the dirty glasses from
the smoke room into the kitchen. Mom and Dad were in their
usual place and there were no adverse comments about my get up.
When I had assembled a fair quantity of dirty glasses in the sink,
I began to wash them up automatically. If I saw dirty crockery I
had to wash it up, I could not help myself.

Standing at the sink up to my arm pits in washing up water I
thought, 'This is bloody stupid, I might just as well be at home.'
Then the back door of the pub opened and three lads walked in.
Carol Pugh had told me they were relatives down from Newcastle
for the week, but had not mentioned they were teenagers, maybe
just a bit older than me.

"Hey, your name Brigitte then?", one of the lads called out. I
ignored them and got on with the washing up.
"Take no notice of him love, what is your name anyway?", asked
his mate.
"Carole, if it's any of your business.", I replied without looking
at them.
"Carole? That's a nice name, would you like a little drink then?"

I turned to face them and saw they were all sitting down and had
small glasses in their hands that held some clear liquid.

"No thanks", I said and went back into the pub to get more
glasses.

When I came back with the loaded tray, the lads were discussing
the day's football results and seemed to have lost interest in me.
I crashed the glasses into the sink and got their attention again.

"Are you sure you won't have a little drink with us love?", asked
the one sitting in the armchair by the fireplace.
"What is it then?" I asked cautiously.
"Oh it's just some pop an' stuff, it won't hurt you, we're all
drinking it." He held out his glass for me to sniff, but there
was no smell.
"All right, just a bit then", I agreed.

On of the other lads handed me a nearly full glass of the 'pop
and stuff' and I took a sip. It tasted horrible, but I did not
let on and took another sip. I did not want them to think I was
not used to drinking in pubs, but the only alcohol that I had had
up until then was a sip from Dad's jug of mild ale on the way
back from the outdoor.

 "All right is it?", he asked.
"Yeah, it's OK.", I told him and drank some more.
"Sit down and have a rest, why don't you?", asked his mate. I
looked around the room but there were no more chairs.

"You can come and sit here, if you like. On my lap.", he patted
his knees invitingly. Oh well, I thought, I had to sit somewhere.
I went over and plonked myself down on him, leaning back against
his chest. He seemed well pleased and filled my glass up again.
The 'pop and stuff' was tasting better and better and I was
feeling quite hot. I drained my glass again.

141

"She's a real boozer this one.", said my new friend, and his mate refilled my glass while we all laughed at the joke. After another few minutes of talking and laughing, my glass was empty again and the lads all cheered me as I held it out for a refill. Here I was, on a Saturday night, in a pub, on a boy's lap and drinking 'pop and stuff' by the glassful. This was really living. If only Mom could see me now.

Then suddenly, the room seemed to tilt sideways and my head began to swim. I was not in the least bit worried by this, in fact, I thought it very funny and started to laugh. Then the lads started to laugh and this made me laugh even more. I was laughing so much I was finding it hard to get my breath. Then I noticed that the boy on whose lap I was sitting was kindly massaging my breasts to help me. The other lad was sitting on the floor with his head on my lap, while the third was trying to stop me laughing and drinking long enough to kiss me. Weren't we all having a great time?.

Just then the door opened and Mom walked in. Even with the room leaning crazily and in fits of hysterical laughter, I recognised her straight away. But when she crossed the room, she looked like a sailor on a storm tossed ship at sea, and this made me laugh even harder, flopping around helplessly all over that boy's lap. Then I heard Mom's voice from somewhere above.

"What the fuckin' 'ell's gooin' on 'ere then?", in a tone that said she knew very well what was going on. Then Mom's face appeared right in front of me and she was sniffing.

"She's fuckin' drunk.", was her verdict. The lads had frozen and wisely said nothing as Mom grabbed my pony tail and yanked me off the chair and off that boy. She did not let go until we reached the smoke room door where she called out to Dad.

"Alf. Alf. She's fuckin' drunk - tek 'er 'ome fer Chrissake. " I felt Dad's hand under my arm and heard his voice from far away. "C'mon gell, let's get ya 'ome." The rest, as they say, is silence.

I woke up in bed some time on Sunday morning still dressed in my rock'n'roll skirt and off the shoulder blouse. They were stained all down the front with dried vomit. Ugh. I was glad that I had been unconscious when it happened. Then I saw Joyce and Linda

1. Dad's first car. Austin 10?

2. Dad with the Hunts in later years. Dad's cigar shows that his business was starting to prosper.

3. Mom and Dad in later years at Stourport.

staring at me from the doorway, looking as though they had been up and dressed for hours.

"You wus drunk last night, our Carole.", they grinned at me. I shooed them away, not needing anybody to remind me. I looked around the room for my Sunday School Bible, intending to swear there and then that I wouldever again drink anything alcoholic or go into a pub. Better still, I would never go within five miles of a pub if only the sickness in my stomach and banging in my head would go away, but it wouldn't.

I only just made it into Mom's room, where the sight and smell of the half full slop pail quickly helped me get rid of the last of the neat gin the lads had been feeding me. Much later, as I sat in our kitchen trying to pour a cup of tea with trembling hands, Mom told me

"That's the last time you do any baby sittin'." For once I did not argue with her. You might be wondering about the baby, the cause of all the trouble you might say. Was he left alone screaming in his little cot all night? No, because when Mom had told the lads what she thought of them, she took over my duties. Naturally, she took the money as well.

Certificate X

"Ah sure, your just gonna 'ave to give that gell a bit more freedom Nance, or you'll lose 'er, so you will." Liza Hunt was trying to put in a good word for me shortly after the babysitting fiasco, when I was again confined to our kitchen on Saturday nights and every other night. Even Betty Hunt, who had as many chores as me, was allowed to go to dances and round to friends' houses in the evenings, but not me. Mom had been quite indignant when Liza mentioned it.

"It ain't me Liza, it's 'er Dad, he wunt 'ave it." But she must have said something to him because it was about this time that they started to take me with them to the Railway Club in St Vincent Street, where they always went on Sunday nights. It was a working man's club and the beer was cheaper than in the pubs, but what really thrilled me about these unexpected outings was that they had live music. There was an elderly trio of piano, drums and bass, and all night they would swing between popular

tunes and old time dance numbers. They were not quite Johnny
and the Hurricanes, but they were loud and (after a few drinks)
quite lively.

I was still working for Mrs Goodman and had plenty of clothes
that I had never had the chance to wear. But my outfits for
these Sunday nights at the Railway Club had first to undergo
Dad's scrutiny and meet with his approval.

Her would be shaving at the sink in the kitchen and I would
come downstairs and parade around while he looked me over.
Then he would give me his considered opinion on my fashion
sense in his inimitable way.

"That fuckin' skirt's too short, they'll see yer arse when yer
bend down." Back upstairs I would go to pull the waistband
of my skirt down a couple of inches.
"Put a vest or summat under that, yer can see all yer whatsit,
at the back." This meant my bra.
"Dad, I don't wear vests anymore an' it's too
'ot in there fera jersey."
"Well, put a cardigan or summat over it then."
"I 'aven't gorra cardigan Dad."
"Yer mother'll 'fuckin' lend yer one wunt she?"
"I ain't gonna wear one of 'ers." I would run back upstairs
muttering to myself, 'One of these soddin' days..'.

I did find a cardigan, one I had had since about age 12 which
was much too small, but I slipped it on anyway and looked in
the mirror. The effect was quite interesting. Under the clinging
material my tits looked even bigger than they had in the blouse.
But wait a minute, you could see the line of my bra underneath,
that was no good. I slipped off the bra and rebuttoned the cardigan. This time the effect was sensational. You could clearly
see my nipples jutting out through the thin nylon. If I walked
into the Railway Club like that I would drive the boys up the
wall.

"Are you fuckin' ready yet?." Dad's voice boomed up the stairs.
I took a last look and settled for a check shirt that buttoned up
to the neck with a bra underneath, of course. Brigitte Bardot on
the Riviera might get away with it, but not Carole Biddle at the
Railway Club.

For a time these Sunday night outings into the great world outside Alexander Street went well. There was the music, a glass

of Babycham if Dad was in a good mood, and plenty of boys
to look at and to look at me. I still had to sit with Mom and
Dad at their table all night, moving only to go to the ladies.
Occasionally they would have a talent contest, and with Mom's
encouragement and Dad's grudging consent, I would get up and
do a song. Years of singing along with the radio and gran's old
records in the front room stood me in good stead, and I would
usually win a prize of perfume or a box of chocolates. One
night, after two glasses of Babycham I sang *Once I Had A
Secret Love.* As I collected my bottle of perfume I was
surprised to see Dad applauding enthusiastically. Doris Day
was still his favourite singer.

When we got home that night, I started my usual tidying up routine when I heard Dad come back downstairs. He had forgotten
to take the wallet from his jacket pocket, as he always kept it
by the side of the bed. Then I noticed his fumbling in the side
pocket of his coat and he came over to me, lifted my hand and
put two half crowns into it.[2 x 12.5p]

"'Ere y'are gell, buy yerself summat.", he said quietly. I was
puzzled, this was a side of Dad I had never seen before. Suddenly
his hand went up to my face and I flinched, half expecting a slap.
But he just ran his fingers down my cheek and I could feel how
callused and rough they were from all the years of metal bashing.

"You're a lovely lookin' gell.", he began.
"Alf, are you comin' ter fuckin' bed then?" Mom's voice from
the bedroom broke the spell and Dad moved quickly away from
me. At the door he paused,
"But it's gonna get ya into a lorra trouble." Then he was gone.

"How much did yer Dad give ya last night then?", were Mom's
first words the next morning.
"You what?"
"You 'eard, 'ow much did 'e give yer last night?"
"Five bob, warrabout it?" [25p] She held out her hand.
"Well, gimme half a crown, [12.5p] I'm short for the dinner
munney."

It was not as bad as it sounds. If Dad had given me half a crown
she would not even have mentioned it, but five bob she considered
too much. Five bob was two days' food money and she was right.

After a few more visits to the Railway Club and more of Mom's
nagging, Dad reluctantly agreed that if any boy asked me I could

get up and dance, and lots of them did. Of course, it was on the strict understanding that I came straight back to the table when the music finished. There was one particular lad that I really liked the look of. He had dark hair, blue eyes and was always smiling and waving to me across the dance floor, but he never asked me to dance. Mom tried her best to help me out. One night when Dad was outside in the gents room, Mom told me her plan.

"When yer Dad comes back, tell 'im yer gooin' to the lavvy, and when that lad sees yer outside, I'll bet he'll come an' talk to ya." Brilliant, why didn't I think of that? When Dad got back, we went through our usual routine as I started to get up.

"Where you gooin' then?"
"Out ter the lavvy Dad", I told him waiting for the nod.
"Goo with 'er will ya Nance?"
"Oh Alf, I don't wanna goo, she'll be all right."

Mom's scheme was working well. As soon as the dark boy saw me he came over. He had a nice line in chat.

"I thought yer wus tied to that bleedin' table.", he grinned.
"'Course I ain't, what's it ter you anyroad?"
"Nothin', just wondered that's all. Wanna come outside fer a bit then?"
"Yeah, all right then, just fer a bit", I answered coolly, but my heart was pounding. For the next few minutes we stood happily outside the main entrance to the club chatting away, him about his vast collection of rock'n'roll records, and me pretending I knew them. The romance was going well.

"Wanna come ter the pictures on Friday? Brigitte Bardot's on with Frank'stein." But I wasn't that daft.
"Brigitte Bardot in a Frank'stein film, gerroff."
"Naw, she's on with it. There's Frank'stein and summat about God mekin' women or summat."

He made it sound fascinating but before I could give him an answer one way or the other, I saw his friendly smile turn into a frozen grin. Standing in the doorway was Dad, watching us. Either he had suddenly become incontinent or he had come out looking for me. I soon found out which it was.

147

"What the fuck yer doin' out 'ere?" he growled.

"Jus' gettin' some fresh air Dad," blushing furiously with embarrassment. The dark haired boy looked bemused and kept
quiet. "Well, get back in" he ordered, jerking his thumb
towards the door.

I did not want to add to my embarrassment by getting a slap
on the ear, so I went, fretting and fuming. He was at it again,
treating me like some 5 year old. And we were not even touching. The expression on my face must have told Mom what had
happened, but all she could do as Dad loomed up was to shrug
her shoulders and roll her eyes to heaven. She had tried her
best for me but now the evening was drawing to a close. The
lights dimmed and the trio struck up with *Who's Taking You
Home Tonight?* A few clinging couples began to slide around
the floor, but the expression on Dad's face made me silently
pray that no boy would ask me for the last dance. The band
droned on, *Who's Taking You Home Tonight?*. If I was not
careful it might be the Saint John's Ambulance team.

When we got home this time, there was no five bob or tender
scene. As they clumped up the stairs, I heard Dad say,

"I ain't tekin' 'er agin Nance, she's fuckin' boy mad, she is."
"Oh leave 'er alone for Chrissake Alf, she's fuckin' young ain't
she?"

But in spite of Mom pointing out the blindingly obvious, there
were no more Sunday nights at the Railway Club. Ah well, back
to the washing up, the spotty Herberts and *Wagon Train*. At least
Flint McCullough would keep me company next Sunday night.

Mom did not give up easily and now seemed determined that
I should have at least a semblance of social life beyond chores,
church, school and work. Ever since their courting days Mom
and Dad had gone to the pictures on Friday nights. Now that
Dad had his little second hand car they would often drive to the
Futurist or Scala Super Cinema in the City centre. Often they
would tell me about the films they had seen, and if they sounded
interesting and were 'U' certificates, I would look out for them
at the Lyric.

One Friday night they did not seem very keen on the film they
had seen, but they went on and on about the film for the next
week. The the trailer had looked really frightening. It was
Alfred Hitchcock's *Psycho*. I started to lose interest when Dad

said it was an 'X' certificate and no one under 16 could get in.
Then Mom said,

"Alf, why don't we tek our Carole with us next week ter see it?
She looks 16 when she's dressed up, don't she?" I waited breath-
lessly for Dad's answer as he looked from Mom to me and back
again, wondering if we had planned this behind his back. Then
at last.

"Yeah, all right then, but only if she's fuckin' ready in time."
Great, my very first 'X' certificate film. For years I had been
wondering what 'X' films were really like. Would it be all blood
and guts? Did the actors and actresses really take off all their
clothes? Now I was going to find out.

Give Dad his due, we really did it in style that Friday night.
We had the plush balcony seats at the Futurist that cost seven
and six each [37.5p], and during the interval we even had a drink
on a stick and Butterkist popcorn. But it was the film that I had
come to see, and I don't think I took my eyes off the screen even
once. I was thrilled, fascinated, frightened and hooked. From then
on horror films became my staple film diet, but *Psycho* is the only
one where I saw whole rows of people almost jumping out of their
seats with fright.

Now I knew that I looked old enough to get in for 'X' films, I
started to go regularly to the horror double bills that were on
the Futurist most Sunday afternoons. One by one I tried all the
other city centre cinemas and was enthralled by their atmosphere.
The thick pile carpets, seats with padded arms, the ever changing
patterns of coloured lights on the heavy drapes before the show,
the framed photographs of famous stars that lined the foyer walls,
and always that sweet scented warm smell. Clutching my copy of
the *ABC Film Review* bought at the pay box for a shilling [5p], I
would enjoy nearly three hours of assorted monsters, werewolves,
vampires and mad doctors.

Sitting alone in that clinging darkness, I watched films like
Blood Beast Terror, Attack of the Slime People and *The Brain
Eaters,* digging happily into my raspberry ripple but never taking
my eyes from the screen. I even loved the adverts, particularly
the one where the fat old fairy waved her wand and a batch of
freshly made pies turned a lovely golden brown. And the trailers,
giving tantalising glimpses of next week's attractions that always
looked better than the ones you had just paid to see. It was all
so unlike our local flea pits with their hard seats, bare floor

149

boards and smelly lavatories. This was the real cinema, sheer magic.

Boys were always asking me to go to the pictures with them, but I always refused. Mom would have let me, but we had to make up stories and excuses for Dad. It was not worth the hassle, especially if he found out. Besides, I liked to watch the film, not snog all the way through. Kissing still seemed stupid and pointless, although I was now fairly certain that it would not make you pregnant. Going alone also had disadvantages. I got fed up with middle aged men sitting down beside me when the cinema was almost empty. Once I had plunged my lighted cigarette into the back of a hairy hand that rested casually on my knee. The man jumped up without a sound and hurried from the cinema.

Eventually, I persuaded our Joyce to go with me on Sunday afternoons. She was still only 13 but wore glasses which made her look much older. If I did her make up and dressed her in Mom's best coat and head scarf, she could get in for an 'X' film. Of course, our make up had to come off before we got back home. Joyce was not very interested in horror films, but if I paid for the tickets and bought her a Velvet Lady, a three flavoured tub of soft ice cream, she would condescend to come. Linda was now old enough to take on my washing up duties, but I had to give her half a crown. This horror film addition was getting really expensive.

We would get off the bus in Corporation Street and walk along New Street, then near the main Post Office, cut down Pinfold Street. One Sunday we had just turned into this short cut when we were stopped by two young men. They were very dark skinned and one had a camera slung around his neck. It seemed that they were foreigners.

"You two pretty girls, yes? We take picture, yes?" Smiling he held up his camera. What possible harm could there be in having our photo taken in the street in broad daylight? Joyce and me stood arm in arm grinning at the camera and the picture was duly taken. Then the one with the camera said,

"We send you picture in post, yes?"
"You give us address to send, yes?", smiled his friend. This was now getting decidedly dodgy. Surely Dad had said something about not giving our address to strangers?
"We go back home tomorrow, we send picture in air mail, yes?"

Oh well, that was all right then, they did not even live in this country. I gave them the address and we parted. On our way to the Futurist we glanced back a couple of times and were quite disappointed that the men were not following.

About two weeks later, early on a school morning, Joyce, Linda and me lay in bed, waiting as usual until the last possible moment to get up. Often Dad would yell up the stairs, 'You lot fuckin' gerrin' up then?' I would lean out of bed and bang my shoes around on the floor to satisfy him we were on the move. But this morning we had gone through shouting and shoe banging, and suddenly Dad was clumping upstairs. We all jumped at once, shoving heads into blouses, looking under the bed for our underwear and pushing feet into shoes. The bedroom door flew open and Dad came in. He was holding a small blue envelope with coloured stripes around the edge, and pulled something from it which he threw onto the bed.

"What the fuckin' 'ell's this then?", he asked menacingly. We all stared down at the little black and white photograph and my heart sank. There were Joyce and me, arm in arm grinning in Pinfold Street. Joyce gave me a sharp nudge in the ribs. It was a 'think of something quick' nudge.

"Er, it's a photo Dad", was all I could come up with.
"I know it's a fuckin' photo, but just 'oo took it, that's what I'm askin' ya." Dad was struggling to keep his temper.
"Er, well, it was these blokes."
"Blokes. What fuckin' blokes? Where?"
"Up in town Dad ... it was these blackies." Dad's eyes almost popped from his head.
"Blackies. Blackies. What fuckin' Blackies?" I babbled on desperately.
"They was on 'oliday, an' they wanted to tek a photo, an' they said they'd send it, 'cause they was goin' back."
"Gooin' back where?", Dad wanted to know.
"Don't know Dad", I was forced to admit. Then the sixty four thousand dollar question.
"An' 'ow did they fuckin' know what address ter send it to then?" Joyce had started to snivel, she knew what was coming.
"I give it to 'em Dad.", I whispered. The slap knocked me back onto the bed and brought stinging tears to my eyes.
"'Ow many times 'ave I told ya never ter give yer address to anybody, how many fuckin' times eh?"

Several dozen at least, but there were more questions. Had we seen the men before or since? Where had we been going and why? Did we always stop and talk to strange men when we went out?

In his outrage Dad forgot to destroy the offending photograph and I have it still [below], a fuzzy print of two teenage girls, one in a coat two sizes too big, on a long ago Sunday afternoon in Pinfold Street. No, they were not good old days, they were too painful for that, both mentally and physically. But when I come across that faded picture, it always makes me smile, even if my right ear does start to tingle a bit.

1. Grinning in Pinfold Street c1958. The old Post Office is on the right and the Council House in the distance. The tiered building on its left was known as Galloway's Corner.

2. With Linda and Joyce on the back step at Alexandra Street just before leaving home c1960.

Hi Ho, Hi Ho

I had seen *Snow White and the Seven Dwarfs* when I was a
kid and had never forgotten the song of the little men as they
marched happily to their jobs. 'Hi ho, hi ho, it's off to work
we go. With a shovel and a pick and a rhubarb stick, hi ho, hi
ho." Now I was 14, nearly 15, it would soon be my turn to
march joyfully out into the world of work, if not with a rhubarb stick, then merrily swinging my little white handbag. It
was something I had looked forward to for a long time.

As the end of term exams approached in my last year at Follet
Osler School, Mrs McLoughlin called me to her office one morning. I had an idea what was coming. On her desk she had my
attendance record and was busy totting something up.

"Carole, do you know that you've been absent more times than
you've been here?", she asked.
"No Miss", I replied innocently.
"And what was the reason for the past, let me see, three weeks
off?"
"Shingles miss." I had really had them and it was awful, I was
on safe ground now.
"Shingles? Oh you poor thing. I've had them and I know how
you feel."

Then the headmistress went on to look at my work record. I knew
and everybody else knew that I was hopeless at everything except
painting, swimming, cookery and domestic science, but to my
surprise, Miss McLoughlin offered me a solution.

"You know Carole, that if you stayed here an extra term, worked
very hard and did extra homework, with your artistic ability you
stand a very good change of getting through the entrance exam for
Moseley Art College." Art college? This was the first I had heard
of it. Drawing and painting all day long, all through the term,
for me that would be paradise.

"Or do you want to go and work in one of the local factories?",
she asked.
"No miss, I had rather do the art college thing miss."
"Well, talk it over with your parents and let me know." Miss
McLoughlin handed me the college application forms, sighed
over my attendance record and let me go.

At home I showed Mom the forms and tried to explain about the
Art College, what I would be doing there and what sort of job I
could get if I did a three year course, and how much I would like
to do it. But I don't think she really took in what I was telling
her. She pretended to read the forms, but all she knew was that I
was not going to get paid for going to college. 'I'll see what yer
Dad ses', was all she had to say.

I never found out what Dad said, but I could guess, because next
day I found the application forms torn in half in the dustbin. I
suppose that I knew, in my heart of hearts, that no matter how
much homework I did nor how long I stayed on at school, I would
never pass the entrance exam. But what made me furious was that
Mom and Dad would not even talk to me about it, as though my
wishes just did not count.

I was in this frame of mind when a girl at school offered me
her cigarette stub in the lavatories. I took it and have been smoking ever since. As I puffed my first fag and between coughs
I thought, 'Right, that's it.' When I got home I took my beloved
paint box from its hiding place and round to a girl I knew who
had a brand new swimming costume that she didn't want. The
swap was made and art college was forgotten.

But although those stinking factories around us were beckoning,
there was still once chance. I had worked at Goodman's Haberdashery on Saturdays for about four years, and when I told Mrs
Goodman that I would soon need a full time job she immediately
offered to take me on. She was prepared to teach me the haberdashery trade and eventually I would manage the shop. But she
could only offer a starting wage of three guineas a week. [£3.15p]

'That suits me,' I thought, no more worries about finding a job.
But I had reckoned without Mom. She would not hear of me
working full time for only three guineas.

"They're payin' gells like you five or six quid a wick for assembly werk down Wilmots.", she informed me. What chance had art
college or Mrs Goodman got against competition like that? I was
upset and disappointed and showed it, but Mom got the wrong end
of the stick and though I was angry at Mrs Goodman for offering
me such a low wage.

"Well what did yer expect, they're fuckin' Jews ain't they?"
The reality was that I would have been happy to work at the
Goodman's for half that amount. But to keep the peace at home
I said nothing.

Soldier, Soldier

Something else happened at around the time I was leaving
school that took my mind off school and work. I became engaged to be married. It was a surprise to everybody, especially
me. I believed that the man who married me would have to be
like Ghengis Khan, who, if he had his Mongol hordes to back
him up and attacked after the pubs had closed, might just, if he
was lucky, snatch me from Mom and Dad. It is an exaggeration,
but this is how I was starting to feel. At 15 years old I had
never had a proper boyfriend and was practically an old maid.

One morning I came downstairs ready to go to school to find a
slim, dark young lad sitting in our kitchen. 'Good morning', he
said, as I carried my toast through to the front room where our
Joyce was eating hers.

"Oo's 'im then?", I whispered.
"He's gonna werk fer Dad, startin' today." I looked at him with
interest through the open door. He was neat and clean and quite
good looking in a mature sort of way. Moments later I caught
him looking at me with interest. It was not too long before he
asked me out or rather he asked Dad if he could ask me out, and
to my surprise Dad agreed.

His name was John Taylor and he was in the Army. He was on
a long leave and looking to earn some extra money, so Dad had
offered him a temporary job. He played the clarinet in the reg-
imental band and could read music. I had never known anybody
who could read music and was very impressed as I sat and
watched him get a tune out of all those dots and squiggles.

Mom was not happy about our relationship.

"'E's bin around 'e 'as", she warned and added darkly,
"'Bin out in Hong Kong, an' yer know what soldiers get up
to out there?" I did not know, all I knew about Hong Kong was
that it was quite far away, somewhere in China. Anyway, we
started going out together, a 15 year old schoolgirl and a 21
year old regular soldier. I had had the odd date with boys, usually without Dad's approval or knowledge, and knew what they
wanted and expected after a night out. But I was still too scared
to even contemplate sex and always avoided places where things
might get out of hand, such as the backs of cars, dark entries,

155

the back row of the pictures or other people's houses. John Taylor's lodgings in Garbutt Street were added to my list.

Give John Taylor his due, he tried every way short of rape to have sex with me, but I always refused with a mixture of what I hoped was firmness and good humour. I did not want to seem like an hysterical schoolgirl, so I countered his pleadings with lines like, 'No, if Dad finds out we're doin' it, he'll kill us both.', or 'No, if yer get me pregnant they'll chuck me out.', or even 'I'm still under age and they'll put us in prison'. I allowed kissing, there was lots of that, though I was still was not too keen, and I sometimes allowed his hand up the back of my blouse in a vain attempt to unfasten my bra strap. It was a special one with a double press stud fastener for just such occasions. Beyond that John Taylor got nothing. Eventually he changed his strategy and asked me to marry him. I was surprised and flattered, but when Dad had a long and private talk with John in our front room, I began to get cold feet. When he had finished with John, Dad called me in.

"Well, yer know what 'e wants, do yer want ter marry 'im?"
I knew what he wanted all right, and when we were safely engaged he thought I would be bound to give it to him.
"I dunno, Dad", I said, stalling for time.
"What you mean, you dunno? Yer must know."
"Yeah, I s'pose so."
"Suppose so? You either do or yer don't, which is it?"
"Oh yes, all right then." I was getting tired of the questions.
"Look gell, I'm askin' yer, not tellin' yer." Dad was getting fed up.
"Yeah, but not 'til I'm old enough," was all I could think of.

Reluctantly I agreed because I was not ready to give up my new freedom. John gave me a lot of attention and trips out, presents and the status of having a real boy friend. It was all new territory and I was not going to give ground unless I had to. The thought of actually marrying John Taylor scared me to death. Anyway, he would be going back to his unit soon and things would sort themselves out, I hoped. Before he left John bought me a lovely engagement ring with a big diamond that I showed off to everybody. I was getting in deeper, and Joyce and Linda could now always make me lose my temper by asking coyly, 'When we gonna be aunties then, our Carole?' Me, a married woman with kids? Never in the rain of pig's pudding, I promised myself.

The Ring and I

With art college ruled out I did not bother to attend for my last
term at Follet Osler School. I was too grown up for that sort
of thing now, engaged to a soldier and everything, and Mom
was only too glad to have full time help around the house.
Veronica reported to me that on the very last day of term,
when Mrs McLoughlin made her speech of farewell to the
leavers, she had mentioned a girl whose record 'brought
shame on the school'. This girl had hardly attended any
classes and got no results at all in the exams. They all knew
that she meant me. Of course I did not pass any exams, I never
sat any. I did not even bother to collect the reports on my class
work because I knew what they would say. There were always
plenty of jobs going for school leavers round our way, and
it now seemed certain that I would end up in one of those
grimy factories that overshadowed life in Ladywood.

At the end of July, as soon as the schools brok up, Mom
took me to the Education Department in Margaret Street to
collect my National Insurance cards and P45. Now I was fully
equipped to start work. Dad did not employ women in his works,
but he was doing a job for a local firm called Brightachrome,
and he told me they were looking for school leavers to start
right away. I went to the Stewart Street works for an interview
and found myself in line with several other girls who had gone
to Follet Osler school. One of them was Pat Clarke and we
both got jobs that day.

The following Monday morning at 8 o'clock, I started my first
factory job. Brightachrome's main business was chrome plating
of small metal objects, such as parts for cars and bath taps. I
was to work at what they called wiring up, which involved taking
small strips of copper wire from a bath of weak acid and attaching
them by hand to the items to be dipped, or chrome plated. No
gloves or other protective clothing were supplied, so by the end
of that first week my fingers were pock marked with acid burns
and some of them were starting to turn green. At this rate, I
would be down to stumps in a few months. Mom noticed the
state of my hands and told Dad.

"I asked that foreman to give yer a decent job, not messin' about
with fuckin' acid. I'll see 'im tomorrer". Sure enough, at dinnertime the next day, the foreman started me in the testing lab.

157

There was no acid and I wore a smart white coat. But this
move did not go down too well with Pat Clarke and some of my
other mates in the factory. They called me crawler and gaffer's
pet, and they were only half joking.

One morning after the hooter for dinner had sounded I was
fooling about with Pat Clarke.   As we walked past the men's
lavatories, she gave me an almighty shove, I staggered through
the floppy rubber doors and just managed to stop myself falling by
holding on to the wall.   Then I noticed a figure approaching that
seemed vaguely familiar. The foreman? The Managing Director?
Count Dracula? No, much worse than all those. It was Dad, with
the pointing finger and staring eyes,

"What the fuck are ya doin'" he wanted to know. "I'll see you at
'ome."

"You keep away from that Pat Clarke", Dad told me over dinner,
"She's no fuckin' good".
But why Dad, she's me mate", I told him. "What's wrung with 'er?"
"'Arf the blokes in the factory 'ave 'ad her, that's what." I did
not dare ask how he came by this information.

Only the next day I let the same Pat Clarke talk me into taking
the afternoon off and going to the pictures. When we got in the
next morning our clock cards were not in the rack and we had to
go to the foreman's office. He was short and to the point.

"You've got the sack", he told us both.
"Collect yer cards at the office and goo."

However, as I passed his office on the way out, he called me in.
"Carole, you can stay if yer want."
"But what about Pat, can't she come back then?"
"No, only you. Mek up yer mind, do yer wanna stay or goo with
yer mate?" I hesitated. Pat would be waiting for me outside.
Then stupidly, I went with my mate.

"Well, that bloody job dain't last lung.", Mom exploded when I
got home and gave her the bad news.
"Don't worry, I'm gooin' out ter get another one in a minit", I
told her.
"Yeah, you'd fuckin' berra, and afore yer Dad gets back, an'
all."

In those days, almost every factory had a board outside listing vacancies waiting to be filled. That afternoon I got myself three jobs, all in the same street. I went back home to sleep on it and decide which to go to in the morning.

When John Taylor went back to his regiment in Hong Kong he wrote to me two or three times a week. He wrote about plans for our wedding, where we would go on honeymoon and our married quarters, which he said would probably be in Germany. He sent me lots of presents, one of which was a nightdress and negligee of Chinese silk. It was for our wedding night he told me enthusiastically, and he couldn't wait to see me wearing it.

I was hopeless at writing letters and always put off replying as long as decently possible. With every reluctant letter that started 'Dear John', I knew the time was coming when I would have to send him a real 'Dear John' letter. But although I knew very well that I could never marry John, I could not bring myself to tell him so, even by post. I stopped writing in the hope that he might take the hint, but he bombarded me with frantic letters asking what was going on - didn't I love him anymore, had I met someone else? Then a mate of John's, a French Canadian, wrote and told me how upset John was, and that I should really write and give him an answer one way or another. At the end he added that he had seen my photograph and if I really did not want to write to John anymore, then I could write to him instead.

As John's next leave drew closer, I got more and more nervous, dreading having to face him and all the inevitable questions. Why didn't I want to marry him anymore, why had I led him on to think that I would, and so on. And even if I managed to evade and avoid all that, he was bound to ask me for his ring back. My beautiful diamond ring, picked out myself from the window of H Samuels in New Street and worn so proudly for a few short weeks. If it would unbind me from John I would be happy to hand it over, but inevitably, there was a problem - I no longer had the ring. It was lying on a velvet pad in the back room of Garfunkel's pawnshop in Monument Road, and what was worse, the deadline for redemption was fast approaching.

A month or so before, on a Friday night, I had been bragging to Tony about how much money I had picked up that week. With overtime it had come to nearly £10. Even after paying Mom for my keep I still had a good bit left to spend. I did not intend to go out that night but was saving for a good spend up on the following Saturday. Then Tony told me that he was not going out that night

either. This was unusual for him, but I did not suspect that he
had other things on his mind.

Our little television set was getting elderly and starting to give
trouble. We struggled for about an hour to get a picture with the
aerial lead attached to a metal coat hanger, but the only place
the coat hanger produced a grainy picture was when I held it half
way up the stairs, so we gave up. Then Tony had an idea. There
was an old pack of playing cards in the kitchen drawer with only
a couple missing. Why didn't we have a game of Pontoon just to
pass the time? Tony assured me that it was 'jus fer laffs', but
to make it more interesting we would play for pennies. I knew
the game but our Tony was obviously in the Brett Maverick
class, because in less than two hours he had won all my hard
earned wages.

I complained tearfully to Mom when she and Dad came back
from the Nelson, but got no sympathy.

"Serves yer fuckin' right fer playin' with 'im, don't it? Yer
know what 'e's like." But how would I get through the coming
week without money? No cigarettes or bacon sandwiches at work,
no new stockings, no make up and no trips to the pictures, and
I still had to go to work. That night as I undressed for bed, I
caught sight of my engagement ring in its fancy box. John had
paid nearly £100 for that ring and there it was, stuck out of
sight in a box. It was the only thing I owned that was worth
anything and it would be a long time before John came home
on leave.

The next morning before I went to work, I gave Mom the ring,
asking her to take it to the pawnshop and get as much as she
could. She looked doubtful and I had to reassure her.

"It'll be all right. John's not comin' 'ome fer ages yet an' with
me overtime an' everythin' I'll get it out in plenty of time." I
told her that if she took it I would 'see her all right', and she
finally agreed. Although I was working quite close to the pawnshop and had Saturday afternoon off, I did not have the nerve to
take the ring in myself. Mom told me she had got £20. As she
was short herself that week, we agreed to split the money and
each save up £12.10 shillings as soon as we could to make the
£25 needed to redeem the ring.

The days and weeks passed too quickly, the overtime at work
dropped off and I never saved any of my half of the ring money.

And neither had Mom. The day of John's home leave dawned and I went panicking to Mom.

"What am I gooin' ter tell 'im Mom? I can't tell 'im we've pawned 'is ring, he'll goo bloody mad." But Mom was no help. "Tell 'im the truth, if 'e don't like it, he'll 'ave ter fuckin' lump it, wunt 'e?"

Maybe John would just ignore me and never ask for his ring back, I tried to tell myself. But he didn't and he did. That very night as I left the factory I saw him waiting for me, and my heart sank. I was very embarrassed, but he seemed calm and to have accepted that I was not going to marry him. He did ask me if there was anyone else and I told him, truthfully, that there was not. It was just that I was too young to get serious about any-body. He took this well and walked me home. I thought I had got away with it, but as we stood in our yard, he asked for the ring. I could not look him in the face as I told the lie.

"Me Mom took it an' pawned it when she wus short of food money one week." Again John was calm and just asked me when I would be able to get it back. Truthfully I told him I did not know, but as soon as I could. He even offered to give me the money to redeem it, but I was not that much of a rat and was glad later that I had refused it.

Mom and me had two weeks left to raise the necessary £25 and I knew we would never be able to do it. To make matters worse, John began to haunt me, not only to ask about the ring but to ask me to go out with him again. If I did then I would be able to keep the ring 'until I was a bit older'. Mom was getting fed up with the whole thing, sick of the sound of John's name and of me telling her every time there was a knock at the door, 'If it's 'im, tell 'im I've gone out'.

It all came to a head one Friday night when I answered the door thinking it was the tally man. John stood there in a smart new suit and asked if I would go out with him. I made an excuse and he asked about the ring. Suddenly Mom brushed passed me and shoved something into his hand.

"'Ere's yer fuckin' ring, now piss off an' don't come back."

John walked meekly away and I never saw him again. Mom had missed paying all our Friday night creditor friends to get the ring back and get rid of John once and for all.

161

"Ya can pay me back out of yer next few weeks wages", she told me and, of course, I did. "I dunno, the way you lead blokes on you'll come 'ome with yer 'ead under yer arm one of these days.", Mom warned.

*At age 16 just after
leaving home.*

Going Where the Sun
Shines Brightly

I had carefully cut out the picture of Cliff Richard from the previous day's *Daily Mirror*. He looked as handsome as ever with his striped shirt and greased back hair. He had just made his film, *Summer Holiday*, and I had made a point of going to see it alone, without interruptions from Joyce pestering me for a Velvet Lady or boys' groping hands. Cliff and me were alone in the perfumed darkness of the Odeon. My interest in pop music had been rekindled when Cliff came on the scene, and my bit of the wall above the bed where I slept with Joyce and Linda was covered with pictures of my idol. My sisters, in various stages of undress, sat watching me sellotape up this latest addition.

"Yer know our Carole, if Cliff ever come down our street an' saw ya, he'd marry ya, I'm sure 'e would". I turned to look at Joyce, but she wasn't joking. Unfortunately her theory was never put to the test.

This was the day I started my new job, one of the three I had got after being sacked from Brightachrome. I had chosen the one at Bullpits, the [Swan] kettle manufacturers on the corner of Icknield Street and Spring Hill. For assembling electric kettles for forty five hours every week, I got six pounds ten shillings, plus overtime. It did not take long for me to get bored messing with kettle bits all day, and I began to hate the job.

Working full time with chores still to do at home on Sundays, Saturday was my only really free day. But with my engagement to John Taylor finally off, I was young, free and single. I went on dates with one or two lads from Bullpits, but they all expected 'you know what' after paying for a cheap seat at the pictures. I even went out with the boss's son, who at least had the upbringing to try to do it in the back of his car and not the back row of the pictures. But I was still having none of it and told myself that I would wait until somebody like Cliff came along. I had to admit that, in our area, it was not very likely.

There were other diversions. A Jamaican called Archie worked at Bullpits as a labourer and he was the first black man that I had ever spoken to. He was always pleasant and polite but seemed very old; I suppose he was about 40. I used to fetch cigarettes from the shop for some of the men, and Archie

would always give me a couple of his for going. A girl
called Valerie Kempson who had gone to Follet Osler School
worked with me on kettle assembly. She was from another
very large family of twelve or thirteen children and lived in
Garbutt Street, which had the reputation of being one of the
roughest in Ladywood. The joke went round that they were
knocking down the houses in Garbutt Street to build slums.

One morning at the factory, there was no Archie and no Valerie.
It turned out that they had gone off together, and so far as I
know were never heard from again. Valerie was the same age
as me, just 16, and it caused quite a sensation in the works.
In a way, I envied Valerie. She had had the guts to break away
and go off with Archie to live in Birmingham, or maybe he had
even taken her back to Jamaica. Wherever she was, it was better
than life in Garbutt Street. Was I destined, I wondered, to spend
the rest of my life in a kettle factory?

I had resumed my Sunday afternoon trips to the picture houses
in the city centre, but these days I saw mainly romantic films
or teenage musicals like *The Young Ones* and *Summer Holiday*.
Most Sundays I took our Joyce with me so I would not be bothered by men. I was going to say 'boys', but some of the
gropers I had encountered were white haired.

On our way to or from the cinemas, we often called at the Art
Gallery and Museum. I loved the atmosphere of peace and
quiet, the smell of polish and the fact that it was free. I would
send Joyce off to the tea room with the price of an orange
squash and a bun while I wandered slowly through the galleries.
I loved looking at the paintings, especially the blind beggar girl
with the rainbow behind her [by Millais]. But my very favourite
section was Natural History. The sheer size of the crouching
tiger amazed me and made me doubt the accuracy of some of
the Tarzan films I had seen. Nobody could wrestle that to the
ground. I liked to look at the big rock that had amethysts glittering inside it and the giant crab. Once when I was staring into
the case of giant spiders, an attendant brushed against me and I
screamed loudly.

"Don't worry luv, they're all dead y'know," he told me, grinning.

Afterwards I would join Joyce in the tea room for a cup of the
lovely frothy Espresso coffee, which was all the rage. After
several visits to the museum we began to notice small groups of
very odd looking people. The boys all had long hair and beards

and wore dark clothes and sandals. The girls were exactly the same except for not having beards, and they wore black make up around their eyes. Most of them carried rucksacks or bags and looked a bit scruffy, but seemed happy enough as they sat for hours sharing one cup of coffee between five or six.

One Sunday afternoon I was staring at a group of them when our Joyce leaned over and whispered,

"Them's Beatniks".
"Beatniks? What's a Beatnik do then?", I asked, surprised at her knowledge.
"Dunno, but that's what they are", she told me confidently.

We heard that most of them did not have anywhere to live, but were 'on the road' as they called it, sleeping rough around the fountains in Chamberlain Square or anywhere else they could find in the City centre. I did not much like the sound of this because I liked my home comforts, such as they were, and it never crossed my mind that one day soon, I might join them.

When Joyce and I called in at the Art Gallery tea room, the Beatniks always seemed to be there, spending ages over their single cup of coffee. Well, it was warm and dry and only cost them sixpence, [2.5p] about a penny each, to sit there for most of the day. Then one Sunday I noticed a new addition to the group who was quite different from the others. He was a tall, very slim, young chap with short dark hair and a pale, thin face. He stood out amongst those beards and jerseys because he wore a smart dark suit with a tie, and even wore cufflinks in the sleeves of his white shirt. He could not be much older than me, I thought, trying not to stare too much.

The following Sunday the Beatniks were in their usual place, but I was disappointed that the suited one was not there. He came in later to a loud cheer from all his friends. It seemed as though they had been waiting for him to bring them something, as he handed out small packets and some loose cigarettes. Wasn't it nice to be so popular, I thought. I was staring again when he looked up and caught my eye. I turned quickly away and felt myself blushing as he smiled at me.

Fumbling in my handbag, I found a cigarette and stuck it in my mouth. Then Joyce leaned across and whispered,

"Hey, that bloke's lookin' at you". I was scrabbling about in my bag for matches and did not look up.
"'Course 'e ain't, what bloke anyway?"
"'Im over there with them Beatniks, 'im with the suit." she told me gleefully.

Before I could answer her or find my matches, a cigarette lighter miraculously appeared in front of me. I recognised the suit and the cufflinks. 'It's just like on the pictures' I thought, as he flicked the lighter and asked quietly,

"Would you like a light then?" There was no trace of Brummie accent in his soft voice. I did not trust myself to speak and hoped that my hand was not shaking too much as I thrust my cigarette into the flame. I took a long drag and blew out the smoke, playing for time.
"Thanks", I managed to mutter.

When I finally looked up the suited one was smiling down at us, then he pulled up a chair from another table, turned it around and sat across it, arms folded on the backrest. I had never seen anybody do that before. He looked at us with interest, from me to Joyce and back again.

"You two sisters, then?", he asked.
"Yeah, that's right" I told him, surprised that it was so obvious.
"Haven't I seen you in here before?"
"Yeah, we come 'ere sometimes when we've bin ter the pictures.", I told him, avoiding his piercing blue eyes as best I could.
"And what have you been to see today?"
"We've sin *It's Trad, Dad* on the Futurist, 'aven't we?" I tried to bring Joyce into the conversation to give me a break, but all she said was 'Yeah'.
"And what did you think of it?" He was full of questions.
"Yeah, it was good wasn't it, Joy?" She nodded dumbly.
"You like trad jazz then?", he asked, relighting my cigarette which had gone out because I had forgotten to smoke it.
"Yeah, it's great."

I felt confident enough to smile back at him now, but I could not understand why he should be so interested in me. A posh bloke like that with all those friends.

"Ever been to the jazz club at the Woodman?" Again, questions.
"No, I don't think so, why?" I had never heard of the Woodman or been to any jazz club.

166

"Well, I'll have to take you some night", then glancing at Joyce, "Both of you". Just then there was a shout from the Beatnik's table.
"Sorry, I've got to go. See you around." With that he went and joined the laughing group at the other table.

He had not even asked my name or told me his, I realised, he could not have been that interested. And what was it the Beatniks had called him? 'Smike' or 'Spike', or something like that.

The following Sunday I told Joyce that I was short of money and could not afford to pay for her to come with me to the pictures, but she was not quite that much of a dope.

"Gerroff, you're gonna see that bloke, ain't ya?", she said grinning.

I did not even bother with the pictures, but went straight to the Art Gallery tea room. I was on my third cup of coffee before he arrived, again with a loud shout of welcome from the Beatniks. He glanced over at me as he made his way to their table and I could not help blushing. He went through his usual routine of distributing gifts around the table and sat talking for a while. If he did not come over I would die of embarrassment, and if he did I probably would as well.

It must look bloody obvious, I thought, me sitting there on my own in all my Sunday finery with two empty coffee cups in front of me. He would think I was after him or something. I was about to get up and leave when he came over.

"Oh 'ello.", I said, trying to sound surprised. I don't think he was fooled for a moment.

"I'm glad you came today", he said pleasantly. I decided to play it cool.
"Oh yeah, why's that then?"
"'Cause I wanted to talk to you." He sat down, still smiling.
"Talk ter me? Warrabout?" I was feeling bold enough to grin back at him now.
"Oh lots of things", he said airily.
"Such as?" It was my turn for the questions. He fixed me with his blue eyes.
"Well, let's see, what about .. love?" This took me by surprise and I blushed again.

"Don't be so daft." I told him. His eyes widened.
"Love isn't daft. It's .. it's .. "

But before he could tell me what it was, there was a shout from
the Beatniks. They were all getting up, scraping their chairs
back and gathering their rucksacks.

"We're all going up to the Woodman", he told me, getting up.
"There's a couple of good bands on tonight. You want to come
with us?"
"Yeah, all right but ..", he saw my hesitation.
"But what?"
"I gorra be in by ten", I told him shamefacedly. It did not seem
to put him out.
"That's all right, I'll see you back to your bus."
"It's the B82 at the top end of Corporation Street" I told him
quickly, in case the walk to and from wherever the Woodman
was put him off.
"Don't worry Cinderella, I'll get you to the bus before you turn
into a pumpkin, all right?"
"Yeah, all right then", I agreed wondering if he was taking the
mickey.

The Woodman, just around the corner from the Museum, was a
Victorian pub. There were heavy wooden carvings and little
round tables with metal legs. A shiny brass footrail ran round the
bottom of the bar which was backed by huge, gilt framed mirrors.
This was the first time I had seen such a luxurious public house,
John had always taken me to the ones around Ladywood. Sadly,
the Woodman was pulled down in the early 1970s and nothing
remains to show that it was ever there. But on this night I
was thrilled by my first experience of live jazz bands.

In a shouted conversation I learned that my new friend's name
was Graham, but the Beatniks always called him Spike. He was
19 years old but would be 20 in a few months time. True to his
word, he got me to the B82 bus in good time and I arranged to
see him again the following Wednesday evening by the fountains
in Chamberlain Square.

Over the next couple of months Spike showed me a Birmingham
that I never knew existed, the night life of Britain's second
city, or rather the nightlife until 9.45 pm when I had to catch
my bus.

What I did see was a revelation. We heard lots of jazz bands at places like the Woodman, including Kenny Ball and Chris Barber. Spike took me to the Jug O' Punch folk club at the Crown in Station Street, where I met Ian Campbell and his folk group. I was really excited a few years later when Ian got his own TV series called *Barn Dance*. Now I knew a TV star. Spike seemed to know everybody and everybody knew him. We went to the Chapel pub in Great Charles Street and met the Spencer Davis Group and their young pianist, Stevie Winwood. Both of them went on to gain fame on TV's *Top of the Pops*. And, of course, there was the Beatnik community. Despite their appearance, few of them were real drop outs. Most were from good, middle class families and went back to their smart, semi detached parent's homes in Kings Heath or Solihull every night. Few that we knew slept rough.

The favourite meeting place for the Birmingham Beatniks and for Spike and me, was the Greyhound pub in Severne Street. It was managed by an Irishman called Gerry Logan, the facilities were basic and the home brewed rough cider sixpence a pint.[2.5p] Spike and Gerry were old friends and once Gerry took us both down to the cellar to see the fermenting vats of cider. The smell was overpowering, but I noticed something floating on the surface of one of the vats and pointed it out to Gerry. He did not seem surprised and leaning over the edge, pulled out a dead rat by its tail.

"Sure, it gives it a bit o'body", he told us, grinning wickedly. I went off cider for a bit after that.

In all the time I spent in the Greyhound pub over those months, I never bumped into anybody from Ladywood. Then one night, to my surprise and delight, who should walk in but Veronica. She was now a slim, attractive young woman with her big dark eyes, long black hair and a mini skirt. She was in the company of a well built young lad who was obviously drunk. We all knew him, he often got chucked out of the Greyhound for trying to inflict grievous bodily harm on everybody around him after a few pints of Gerry's rough cider. I watched him wobble up to the bar for more drinks, then I turned to Veronica.

"'Ow the fuck did yer get mixed up with 'im then?"
"Met 'im at a party' she told me, smiling fondly over at him.

A few years went by before I saw Veronica again. I bumped
into her in Corporation Street and we went for a coffee in
Lewis's roof garden. Almost the first thing I said to her was,

"'Ere, the last time I saw ya, yer wus with that bloke, what's 'is
name? You know, the one 'oo wus always drunk, an' in punch
ups an' getting chucked out the pub. A right looney 'e wus.
What- ever 'appened to 'im?"
"I married him", Veronica said quietly.

Then I saw what could have been fading bruises under the heavy
make up around her eyes and I got very embarrassed. She came
to my rescue as she had often done when we were kids.
"Don't let's talk about it." she said brightly, so we didn't.

Spike himself was also a revelation to me, so different from any
other boy I had known. Well educated, well spoken and good
mannered, he never took the mickey out of my broad Brummie
twang and seemed interested in everything I said and did, although I could never understand why. He did not pester me
to have sex with him or try to make me do anything I did not
want to. I liked his company and he seemed to like mine. In
short, being with Spike was 'fun', something I had not had
very much of, and there was never the nervous anticipation,
close to dread, that I had felt when dating other boys.

Spike told me that his parents lived in a big house with grounds
in Cheltenham and his father was managing director of the Dun-
lop Tyre factory in Castle Bromwich. He did not live with his
parents but he had his own room, or pad as he called it, somewhere in the City. Casually he told me that he had just returned
from six months living in Paris where he had been writing a book.
Of course, I knew that all boys were liars but there was something
about Spike that almost made me believe him. I never quite did,
not until I actually stood on the lawns of that lovely house in
Cheltenham.

Spike was full of surprises and one night told me that he often
wrote poetry. Poetry. The only poetry I knew then were rhymes
about young ladies from various parts of the country. He showed
me some of his stuff and it looked like proper poetry to me, where
the words at the end of the lines don't rhyme. But he was always
very vague about what he actually did for a living. He went down
to London a lot, he said, to do 'deals'. When I asked what sort
of deals he said, 'Oh, this and that, you know'.

I didn't, though I should have guessed, it was all there in front of me. The little packets and loose cigarettes for the Beatniks, trips to London, deals, popular with everybody, and they called him Spike.

But I was young and in love, and by the time I had known Spike for a couple of months I would have believed anything he told me and forgiven him anything he did. His lifestyle was so different from what I had been used to, a world of pubs, jazz clubs, late night parties and even occasional all night poetry reading sessions. How could I compete with that when I still had to be in by 10 o'clock every night? It was gnawing at me.

Every time Spike left me at that bloody B82 bus stop he would go straight back to the high life we had just left, back to the Beatniks and those pale, dark eyed girls. In desperation I broached the subject with Mom.

"Why can't I stay out 'til 11 now I'm 16?" She looked at me suspiciously.,
"Why do yer wanna stay out that late anyroad?"
"Well, the jazz club don't finish 'til 11 and I always 'ave ter come out before the end."

"Ten o'clock's late enough fer a gell of your age an' nothin' good ever 'appens after ten." So there it was. I knew that the crunch would come sooner or later, but it came sooner than I expected.

By now I had discarded my off the shoulder blouses with flared rock'n'roll skirts and got myself a Beatnik outfit. It was a black jersey three sizes too big, and some second hand jeans from the rag market, which I tried to make tighter by having a bath in them. I had started using black eye liner and brushed my light brown hair out long and straight. I had mentioned Spike at home. Well, I had more than mentioned him. According to Mom and my sisters, I was going on about him all the time. 'Spike? Spike? What sort of a name is that? An' 'oo the bloody 'ell is 'e anyroad?', Mom had wanted to know. But how could I tell her that he was the most wonderful person that I had ever met, that I was madly in love with him and desperate to spend the rest of my life in his company.

Spike's 20th birthday was looming and there was to be a night of celebrations. We were to meet all our friends in the Stage Door coffee bar in Needless Alley at 7 o'clock, go on to the

171

Greyhound until closing time, then on to Stourport for an all night rave in the caves on the river bank. But, of course, by then I would be riding the smoke filled B82 heading back to the mean streets of Ladywood. I had never been to an all night party or known anybody who had, but Spike urged me to tackle Mom and Dad about it.

"Tell them that I'll look after you and bring you back safe the next morning."
"You come an' tell 'em yerself." I replied, knowing what the reaction would be. But Spike had never been to our house in Alexander Street and I was not keen that he ever should. It might put him right off me when he saw where I came from, but I was prepared to take that chance if he could persuade Mom and Dad to let me go to his party.

"No, I don't think I will Carole, if you don't mind, parents always want to know too much about their daughter's boyfriends, don't they?"

I pictured Mom and Dad firing questions at him. Where did he work? What was his job and what exactly went on at all night parties? I did not press him any further and decided to tackle Mom myself. Her response was as short as it was predictable.

"All night fuckin' party? Huh. You can ask yer Dad an' see what 'e ses if yer like." I had known it was a waste of time.

My birthday present to Spike had been a Beatnik style jersey of black wool, and he was wearing it as we sat in the Stage Door coffee bar waiting for our friends to arrive. He had let his hair grow longer and was even wearing jeans. I thought he looked gorgeous, blue eyes sparkling, as he greeted everybody with a laugh and joke. But I was not feeling in the party mood as I sat sipping my espresso and watching the time. In a few short hours, I would have to drag myself away from all this and head home, leaving Spike to the all night party and those all night Beatnik girls. It was really more than flesh and blood should be asked to stand. But I cheered up a bit when we got to the Greyhound and everybody sang Happy Birthday to Spike. Gerry Logan gave us a round of free drinks and Spike even bought a bottle of Champagne that we shared between us. Another first for me.

As the night wore on, I drank more than I had ever done before, more even than the night baby sitting at the Nelson. The juke box was blaring out the Beatles's *Love Me Do* for most of the night, as I sank pint after pint of Gerry's rough cider hopefully unflavoured by essence of rat.

Time passed in a whirl of music, smoke, cider fumes and laughter. It was quite a shock when I heard Gerry call 'Time gentlemen please.' It was almost 10.30 and I had missed my bus. There would not be another until nearly 11.00 and by the time I got home it would be getting on for half past. Mom and Dad would have been in for ages, and I was reeking of drink. There was going to be one almighty row, and even a good old fashioned belting was not out of the question.

Outside the Greyhound I started to panic and told Spike he would now have to come home with me and explain to Mom and Dad why I was so late. But he had had a lot to drink as well and was not too concerned about my predicament.

"Don't worry about it. What can they do? Kill you?" But he did not know how close to the truth he was. I got hysterical. "Spike, I'm not gooin' back there on me fuckin' own, you've gorra come with us or I ain't gooin back."
"Okay, okay. Calm down. I'll come back with you and explain, then it'll be all right, you'll see."

I prayed that Mon and Dad had come in late that night. I was not old enough to have my own front door key, and if they had gone to bed and we had to knock them up ...

As we walked along Alexandra Street towards the house I began to feel really sick. The champagne, cider and the cool night air were taking effect and I leaned heavily on Spike. When we got to the house it was in darkness and my heart sank.

"Oh fuck, they've gone ter bed. What we gonna do now?" I asked him in real alarm.
"Knock on the door.", he suggested calmly.
"You don't know what they're like when they've 'ad a drink.", I hissed at him.
"Well, I'll knock it then" he said, and moved towards the door.
"No.", I screeched, "Come away or they'll 'ear us."

I was standing just inside the entry leaving against the wall and wondering how I could wake our Joyce without disturbing Mom and Dad. Spike came into the entry.

"Look, I can't stay here all night. They're waiting for me at .."
"Well fuck off them, if that's what yer want. Fuck off an' leave me 'ere."
"It's not what I want, but you can't stay in the entry all fucking night, can you?" It was the first time I had heard Spike swear and it made me jump.
"Jus' don't knock that door" I pleaded. "Jus' shurrup an' let me think fer a minit, will ya?" My head was swimming and I could see Spike was getting fed up with hanging about. He looked at his watch.

"It isn't even half eleven yet. So you're late. What can they do to you anyway?", he asked reasonably. We did not wait long to find out.

Suddenly the front door crashed open and Dad was there, trousers pulled over his pyjamas and barefoot. He grabbed Spike by the lapels of his suit jacket and growled,

"So you're fuckin' Spike are ya?" He then proceeded to try and punch him senseless. I screamed at Dad and tried to get between them, Spike pulled away, the sleeve of his jersey tearing. Then Mom appeared, screaming at me to get in the house and leave them to it, and behind her the wide eyed faces of Joyce and Linda. The tow was terrible. Lights came on across the street and a window opened.

"Will ya shut that fuckin' noise up, I gorra get up fer werk in the mornin', so I have." It was one of the Irish lodgers from opposite.
"Mind yer own fuckin' business." Dad bawled back.
"You mek enough fuckin' row when yer come 'ome pissed." Mom pointed out at the top of her voice. Spike took advantage of this diversion to grab my arm,
"C'mon, they're all fucking mad around here. Let's go." We ran.

The shouts and screams followed us until we turned the corner and paused for breath. Spike stared at me, white faced.

"I can't believe it", he gasped. Of course, this familiar Saturday night scene was completely alien to him. I couldn't help giggling at his shocked expression, despite the fact that I only had the clothes I stood up in and a pair of Joyce's shoes which I had borrowed for the evening.

"I told yer, didn't I?" Then he grinned and it was all right.

My hands were trembling as I dialled our number from the phone box outside the Museum, but I did not feel sick any more and I was almost sober. They would all have gone back to bed by now, so I let it ring. At last, I heard a low, scared voice from the other end.

"'Ullo, 'oo's that?", asked Joyce.
"It's me an' I'm not comin' back.", I said in as firm a voice as I could manage.

"Carole? What you mean yer not comin' back?", Joyce asked in alarm.
"What I say. I'm gooin ter live with Spike, you tell Mom an' Dad in the mornin'".
"Oh Carole, yer can't." She sounded really upset.
"Yes I bloody can. You tell 'em I'm not comin' back - ever."
There was a long silence.

"Well, warrabout me shoes then?"
"Fuck yer shoes." I told her and slammed the phone down.

That was just typical of our Joyce, me leaving home and all she was worried about was her rotten shoes. They were hurting me anyway.

I looked out through the greasy panes of the phone box window and saw Spike sitting on the edge of the fountain, staring into the gushing water. What did I really know about this young man who I prayed would now want me with him all the time? Not a lot, but I knew I loved him and that was good enough for me to be going on with. I pushed open the phone box door and the Museum clock, Big Brum, began to strike 12.00. I had never been out in the street this late before and it was a good thing I had never heard that quotation about tolling bells, or I might have had second thoughts.

Spike looked up as I approached.

"All right?", he asked.
"Yeah - but I ain't gooin' back there" I said, watching his face.
"Have you told them?" I was thankful he did not seem put out.
"Yeah, well I told Joyce an' she'll tell Mom an' Dad in the mornin'."

"What do you think they'll do then?", he asked, as if he really wanted to know.

"Dunno, not much they can do is there? I'm over 16 ain't I?" I noticed the torn sleeve of his jersey where his white shirt was showing through. I put out my hand, ran my fingers along the tear and Spike looked down at it ruefully.

"I can sew that fer ya", I told him.

"Can you?" He seemed genuinely surprised.

"'Course I can. Come top in sewin' at school." School seemed very far away now, but if I could mend Spike's jersey, it would not all have been a waste of time.

"Well, what do you want to do now?", he asked looking back at the water.

"Goo with you ter Stourport", I told him without hesitation.

Spike looked at me seriously for a moment.

"Are you sure?"

"Yeah, I'm sure." He got up, smiled and took my hand.

"Good. Come on then, let's go." His hand was warm and comforting as we walked back to Corporation Street and the all night bus that would take us to Stourport.

The sun had always seemed to shine when we had camped out at Stourport, so perhaps it was a good omen that Spike and me would

be starting our life together there. Perhaps it would be like I had seen it in *Summer Holiday*. As Cliff put it:

> 'We're going where the sun shines brightly,
> We're going where the sea is blue,
> We've seen it in the movies,
> Now let's see if it's true.'

I had watched the scene that me and Spike were playing lots of times in films. Boy and girl walk off into the sunset to a happy life of domestic bliss. Could it ever, did it ever, come true in real life I wondered? Well that, as authors say with their eyes on a second book, is definitely another story.